THE
ORDINARY
LEADER

10 KEY INSIGHTS
FOR BUILDING AND LEADING
A THRIVING ORGANIZATION

RANDY GRIESER

ACHIEVE
PUBLISHING

Published by ACHIEVE Publishing
62 Sherbrook Street, Winnipeg, Manitoba R3C 2B3
www.achievecentre.com

Bulk discounts available. For details contact:
ACHIEVE Publishing at 1-877-270-9776 or info@achievecentre.com

This book is typeset in Minion Pro and Brandon Grotesque.
Printed with vegetable-based inks on 100% PCW paper.

ISBN: 978-1-988617-00-8
ISBN: 978-1-988617-01-5 (ebook)

Printed and bound in Canada
First edition, second printing

Book design by Ninth and May Design Co.

10 9 8 7 6 5 4 3 2

For Heidi, my partner in life,
and for Ben and Ana,
because *why* starts with family.

CONTENTS

• • • • • • • • • • •

INTRODUCTION

● ● ● ● ● ● ● ● ● ● ●

ORDINARY BUT NOT AVERAGE

I am an ordinary leader, and I am not the only one. There are many of us, and while we may be ordinary, *we are far from average.* Between us, we ordinary leaders lead the majority of the world's workforce. We lead many small organizations and teams that do great things.

Most ordinary leaders don't follow all the neat and tidy formal norms. I, for one, don't wear a tie, my desk looks like a hurricane hit it, and I chew on the end of my pen while I'm thinking. The files on my computer are a mess – I have one main folder that runs on and on.

I have my fair share of weaknesses (see Chapter 4 for full disclosure). I don't hide them or pretend they are not there. Absolutely, I am exceptional in some areas, but in others, not so much. I see myself, quite simply, as an ordinary leader. Yet I'm anything but average, and the organization I lead is extraordinary!

WHO ARE ORDINARY LEADERS?

In using the term "ordinary," I am referring to me, and likely you –

ordinary leaders of small organizations and teams. We are not leading large corporations or big government agencies. Nor are we often written about in books or quoted in magazines. We are not Jeff Bezos of Amazon or Howard Schultz of Starbucks. *We are, however, important. Maybe not globally, but in our own realm of influence, our leadership makes a difference.*

Look around you and you will see ordinary leaders everywhere. In the course of a typical day, I might connect with the following leaders:

- My children's principal, when I drop them off at school.
- A client at a lunch meeting, who is a manager at a social service agency.
- The owner of the local bike shop where I pick up supplies for my mountain bike after work.
- A friend I have supper with, who is an executive director of a not-for-profit arts organization.

Most leadership books seem to be written, either explicitly or implicitly, with leaders of large organizations in mind. While the strategies and ideas in those books can sometimes translate to leaders of smaller organizations, the insights often just don't fit. The insights in *this* book, while still applicable to large organizations, are written for and from the perspective of someone leading a small to medium-sized team or organization.

THE EXTRAORDINARY LEADER MYTH

Some people are very quick to name extraordinary leaders based on accomplishments and notoriety. In their eyes, recognizable politicians, athletes, and entrepreneurs are shining examples of leadership.

Yet when you look closely, behind most people the world identifies as extraordinary due to their fame or fortune, you will find an ordinary person whose circumstances are extraordinary.

INSIGHTS AND GUIDING PRINCIPLES

Most leaders I know can clearly identify two or three, perhaps even ten or more, insights and principles that guide them. These are the things they aspire to, strive for, and identify as instrumental to their success.

I have 10 key principles. They are not stand-alone insights. They influence, support, and build on each other. For example, talent and team selection, organizational health, motivation, and employee engagement all rely on one another. Likewise, it is difficult for a leader to excel at creativity and innovation if he or she lacks passion.

The 10 chapters in this book each explore a specific insight.

Chapter 1: Motivation and Employee Engagement

Employee engagement occurs more readily when employees do tasks that bring them satisfaction, when they are given autonomy, and when they work in an organization that makes a difference. Leaders in organizations with high levels of engagement do not view these nonfinancial benefits simply as afterthoughts.

Chapter 2: Passion

Passion, as well as a lack of passion, is contagious. No one has ever been inspired by a leader who is not passionate. If you want to have a passionate, inspired workforce, it must begin with you, the leader. Passion inspires others to join and identify with your vision.

Chapter 3: Vision

Vision gives us a sense of purpose and guides us as we work in the present. Visionary leaders energize and inspire people to work toward a future goal. They are able to clearly and vividly communicate what the future holds.

Chapter 4: Self-Awareness

The ability to be honest with yourself about your strengths, and more importantly, your weaknesses, is essential for leading an organization. Focusing on strengths, while working to mitigate the impact of weaknesses, requires leaders to have a high level of self-awareness.

Chapter 5: Talent and Team Selection

Much of what organizations accomplish can be traced back to employee selection. Taking the time to create the right process for bringing in people who fit both the job and the culture of the organization is essential.

Chapter 6: Organizational Health

Nobody should dread going to work in the morning. To achieve and maintain success, leaders must be vigilant and focused on creating and sustaining a happy and supportive work environment with high employee morale.

Chapter 7: Productivity

Without a focus on productivity, organizations become irrelevant and fail. Productivity, for both individuals and organizations, should always come down to *how* we get things done. It's not just a matter of working hard.

Chapter 8: Creativity and Innovation

It is far more motivating to work in an organization that values creativity and innovation than one that is sterile and stuck. A leader who values innovation creates a culture that embraces and empowers employees to be part of the innovative process in all aspects of the organization's work.

Chapter 9: Delegation

Effective leaders learn to delegate because it frees up time for them to address the tasks that only they can do or that they can do best. Delegation is not merely a way to lighten one's workload; it also serves to increase the motivation and competence of those delegated to.

Chapter 10: Self-Improvement
Great leaders walk through life continuously curious about the way things work. They read as much as they can, listen to new ideas, and meet other people who are doing great things. Self-improvement makes all the other principles easier to achieve.

These insights are not just mine. Most of you will also relate to some of them and identify with them as your own. While these insights are relevant to all leaders, the importance of each principle will vary depending on the nature of each organization and each leader's personality. I present these insights to you with the realization that we are all on a different path – and also with the belief that none of us have arrived.

I am sure that these insights will have evolved for me in 10 years' time, and some new ideas will have emerged. I will have learned new lessons and made more mistakes. *These insights are therefore not exhaustive, set in stone, or complete.*

ORIGINS OF *THE ORDINARY LEADER*
The Ordinary Leader: 10 Key Insights for Building and Leading a Thriving Organization has evolved largely in response to questions I have been asked with increasing frequency in recent years. The questions are usually some version of, "Why has your organization been so successful?" or "What are the principles that have helped you lead and grow your organization?" *The Ordinary Leader* is my attempt to answer these questions.

When I started the Crisis & Trauma Resource Institute and ACHIEVE Centre for Leadership & Workplace Performance, I would not have been able to articulate these 10 insights. I certainly did not start out with these principles in mind, and in reality, this list has evolved over time. A decade later, these 10 insights have proven to be integral to our organization's success.

I, and we as an organization, have grown into these principles slowly. They are now core to my leadership style and our organizational culture, but they have not always been. There have been times when the absence of these guiding insights cost us dearly:

- We have hired the wrong people for the culture we were trying to build, and we have hired the right people but put them in the wrong positions.
- We have allowed conflict between employees to escalate to the point where productivity suffered due to gossip, withholding of information, and sabotage.
- We have stymied innovation and creativity, prohibiting employees from feeling empowered and thus decreasing motivation.

In many ways, the mistakes we have made and learned along the way have helped me recognize these 10 key insights.

MY STORY

My education has led to degrees in theology, conflict resolution, and social work. I have worked in many different fields, including construction, agriculture, organizational consulting, social services, and counseling. Like other leaders I know, my path to leadership has been filled with seemingly random and interesting steps along the way.

Ten years ago, as a way of supplementing my income as a counselor, my wife and I created a brochure to promote two different workshops I had created. We mailed it out to 3,000 organizations that we thought would be interested in the topics. Within four months, I had quit my job and was working full time on our new business.

Five months after we sent these first brochures, we hired our first employee. We have expanded quickly and have added at least one new employee each year. I now lead an organization with 15 employees and close to 100 contract trainers. We have two divisions:

- ACHIEVE Centre for Leadership & Workplace Performance (ACHIEVE) provides training and resources in the areas of leadership development and workplace performance.
- Crisis & Trauma Resource Institute Inc. (CTRI) provides training and resources in the areas of mental health, counseling, and violence prevention.

In addition to offering public workshops, we also offer on-site training, webinars, resource manuals, assessment tools, and consulting.

Over the past 10 years, I have led a team that has positioned these organizations to be two of the premier providers of professional development training in the industry. This could not have been possible to achieve if I hadn't learned to focus on the insights I share in this book. While my own story is embedded in the context of being an entrepreneur, these insights and this book are for all who relate to being a leader.

THE MAKING OF A LEADER

Most of us are familiar with the age-old question: Are leaders born or made? While personality traits and talents can make leading easier for some people, I believe great leadership is developed through a continuous process of self-reflection, education, and experience.

To be an effective leader, there are some things you must know and do, and not all of them will come naturally. Leadership development occurs more quickly and simply when you have a desire to be a better leader, an openness to reflect on your approach to leadership, and a willingness to grow and adjust.

Descriptions of leadership abound, yet certain aspects of leadership are so nuanced that simple definitions rarely do justice to the full meaning of the word. Nonetheless, here is my attempt:

- Leaders inspire and influence others to *willingly* act – they act because they want to, not because they have to.
- Leaders have earned trust, and they are therefore able to influence others to act without using coercion.

These descriptions provide a high standard to live up to, so much so that many of us can only aspire to achieve great leadership. *Interestingly, I have noticed that as long as I strive to be a good leader and acknowledge when I fall short, my staff will forgive me.*

THE IDENTITY OF A LEADER

Strongly identifying as a leader makes it easier to be a leader. Think about it: Do you identify as a leader? When you introduce yourself to others do you say, "Hello, my name is Randy and I own a training company?" Or do you say, "Hello, my name is Randy and I lead an organization that provides training?" Notice the difference? It's subtle. The latter demonstrates first and foremost my identity as a leader, not as an owner or manager.

I have grown into my identity as a leader over time. Early on I struggled to identify as a leader. I could say it was because I felt too young or because I more passionately identified as an entrepreneur. The truth is I wasn't ready to *work* at being a leader.

Leadership requires us to be thoughtful and intentional about what we do and how we do it – it takes time and requires work. Here's an interesting thing that occurs once we identify as leaders: we raise the bar, and we become accountable. Identifying as a leader makes us accountable to ourselves and to those we are leading.

An important aspect of a leader's identity is the ability to articulate one's leadership approach. I encourage you to read this book with curious eyes. As you read, reflect on your own organization and ponder how these insights fit for you. Think about what might change if you were to incorporate some of these insights into your leadership approach.

LEADERSHIP SURVEY RESULTS

In May 2016, our organization completed a survey[1] that gathered opinions and perspectives about the 10 principles that make up the foundation for this book. We received responses from 1,063 leaders and 648 employees.

Insights from the survey are woven into some of the chapters of this book. Quotes from survey respondents can be found in each chapter under the headings "Employee Survey Responses" and "Leader Survey Responses." You can also find additional quotes and insights from respondents in the section of this book called "Survey Responses," on page 172.

The question posed to leaders was:

- Identify *three principles* from the list below that are *most important* for you as a leader.

The questions posed to employees were:

- Identify *three principles* from the list below that are *most important* for you to see in your leaders.
- Identify *up to three principles* below that you feel are *lacking* in your leaders.

The choices listed below were randomly placed in a different order for each survey respondent:

- **Self-Awareness**: Keen awareness of strengths and weaknesses.
- **Vision**: Thinks strategically about the future.
- **Team Selection**: Builds the right team and finds the right fit.
- **Delegation**: Knows what, who, and when to give tasks to others.
- **Passion**: About one's own work and the work of the organization.
- **Productivity**: Articulates and drives the achievement of goals.
- **Innovation**: Focus on creativity and efficiencies.
- **Motivation**: Empowers staff through support, encouragement, and autonomy.
- **Organizational Health**: Cultivates a happy and supportive workplace.
- **Self-Improvement**: Is curious, seeks inspiration, and stays current.

Each respondent was also given space to provide written feedback. The results of the survey are in the next three graphs:

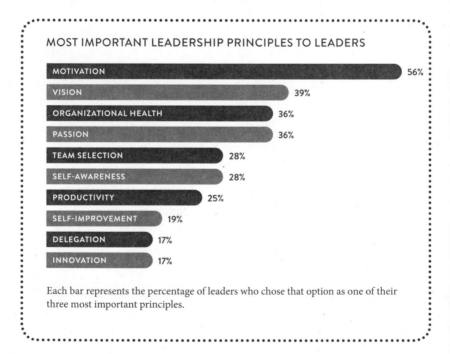

MOST IMPORTANT LEADERSHIP PRINCIPLES TO LEADERS

MOTIVATION	56%
VISION	39%
ORGANIZATIONAL HEALTH	36%
PASSION	36%
TEAM SELECTION	28%
SELF-AWARENESS	28%
PRODUCTIVITY	25%
SELF-IMPROVEMENT	19%
DELEGATION	17%
INNOVATION	17%

Each bar represents the percentage of leaders who chose that option as one of their three most important principles.

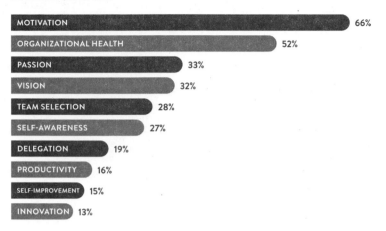

MOST IMPORTANT PRINCIPLES FOR EMPLOYESS TO SEE IN THEIR LEADERS

MOTIVATION	66%
ORGANIZATIONAL HEALTH	52%
PASSION	33%
VISION	32%
TEAM SELECTION	28%
SELF-AWARENESS	27%
DELEGATION	19%
PRODUCTIVITY	16%
SELF-IMPROVEMENT	15%
INNOVATION	13%

Each bar represents the percentage of employees who chose that option as one of their three most important principles.

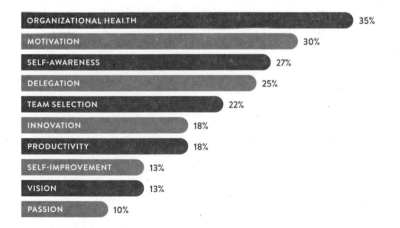

WHERE EMPLOYEES FEEL THEIR LEADERS ARE LACKING

ORGANIZATIONAL HEALTH	35%
MOTIVATION	30%
SELF-AWARENESS	27%
DELEGATION	25%
TEAM SELECTION	22%
INNOVATION	18%
PRODUCTIVITY	18%
SELF-IMPROVEMENT	13%
VISION	13%
PASSION	10%

Each bar represents the percentage of employees who chose that option as a principle their leaders are lacking. (Note that for this question, percentages are lower because respondents could choose up to three principles or none at all.)

WHAT LIES AHEAD

The chapters ahead are placed intentionally in the order in which they appear. The principles impact and overlap with each other, and understanding one principle will often be helpful in fully appreciating the next. Sometimes I make these connections overtly, but most of the time the associations are left to the reader to make. Given that motivation was the principle that both leaders and employees identified as most important, I begin with Motivation and Employee Engagement.

As I researched and wrote this book, I also interviewed 10 other leaders across a range of professions and organizations. You will find their voices in each chapter, identified in sections called "Another Leader's Insights." I can vouch for these leaders. I know them, and I have seen them work. I have had conversations with them about their challenges in leadership and their dreams for their organizations.

I will reference only a few public figures and authors whom I don't know personally. Of these, I chose those whose public speaking and writing indicates that they strive to be strong leaders.

I am used to getting my point across by talking. As a speaker I use tone, volume, and inflection to emphasize my thoughts and ideas. In this book that is not possible, so I've used *italics* instead. When you see a word or sentence in *italics*, that is my way of making that word or sentence stand out.

1

MOTIVATION AND
EMPLOYEE ENGAGEMENT

● ● ● ● ● ● ● ● ● ●

WHAT MATTERS MOST

I begin with this chapter on motivation and employee engagement because our survey results clearly indicate that this is the topic that matters most. Motivation is the highest priority on the minds of both leaders *and* employees.

Of the leaders surveyed, 56 percent identified motivation as one of the top three principles that are most important to them. Likewise, 66 percent of employee respondents identified motivation as one of the top three principles they would like to see in their leaders.

Leaders and employees both want the same thing. This is good news! However, there appears to be a gap between desire and reality. In the same survey, 30 percent of employees identified motivation as one of the top three principles their leaders are lacking. This is the second most common principle identified as lacking in leaders. And the most common, organizational health, directly impacts motivation.

It is clear that focusing on motivation and employee engagement is the key place to start when working to build a thriving organization.

MOTIVATION 101

The root of motivation is motive. *Webster's New Collegiate Dictionary* describes motive as "something (a need or desire) that causes a person to act." Motive is the reason we do some things and not others. We must first become aware of our desire or need and then choose whether or not the task at hand warrants our highest level of dedication. If it does, we choose to consciously work toward completing the task or achieving a goal because it satisfies our needs or desires. Motivation is a committed, conscious choice to act.

People who reach their goals have the courage to first contemplate and name their hopes for the future. The highest level of committed motivation occurs when we choose to do something greater in our lives, whether that means obtaining a higher level of fitness or excelling at our profession. When we aspire to be greater, we consciously choose to work toward that objective.

I know too few people who take the time to truly reflect on why they are motivated, why they get up and do what they do, and what more they want in their lives. On the other hand, I know many people who hope and wish for increased motivation. However, one does not become more motivated by hoping and wishing. *Motivation occurs with a conscious connection to need, desire, and hope, followed by sustained commitment and action – the doing that is required to reach a goal.*

PROGRESS IS MY MOTIVATION

People who know me well often describe me as highly driven and motivated. I am always thinking, doing, and acting. Progress is my motivation. The more progress I make, the more motivated I am to continue. The more attention I give to my goals and passions, the more motivation I have.

It has never been lost on me that my own personal drive, motivation, and engagement are essential to our organization's success. It was because of my initiative that our organization began. However, the motivation and engagement of the people who work in our organization have become equally important. It is our employees who ensure that the activities required for progress are actualized.

SUSTAINED MOTIVATION

Many people are motivated for short bursts of time and then find that their motivation wanes. One only has to look at the increased attendance at fitness clubs each January and then return a few months later to see that many people have not been able to stick to their New Year's resolution fitness goals.

Success is not achieved within periods of fleeting motivation. Goals, dreams, and long-term successes are only achieved while staying motivated for long periods of time. Our ability and desire to get up day after day to pursue our dreams is what separates those of us with high levels of motivation from those who only have fleeting commitment.

The key distinction between sustained and fleeting motivation is disciplined effort. Motivation does not sustain itself. Those who relentlessly pursue their goals and dreams with focused discipline and ambitious effort are the people who obtain sustained motivation. When we give more disciplined effort, we will feel more motivation.

DISCIPLINED AND CONTINUAL EFFORT

I am not a former Olympic athlete or even a high-level athlete. In fact, the highest praise I can give myself while keeping a straight face is that I am slightly above average when it comes to fitness.

Over a decade ago, I participated in an adventure race. It was one of the hardest activities I have ever done. I was on a team of four. The event combined biking, hiking, navigating, and canoeing over a period of 36 hours through rugged wilderness terrain. For the slightly above-average athlete, this is a really long time and a major test of motivation.

I had been committed throughout my preparation for the race, practicing and training harder than I ever had before. Yet I was unprepared for the inevitable point in the race, early in the morning after biking all night, when I simply wanted to quit. I was tired, bloody, hungry, and grumpy. My motivation for completing the task had waned, but I dug down, found my reserve of effort, and continued. Unfortunately, there is no glory at the end of the story: at the 35th hour, we became lost and were unable to complete the race.

The moral of the story is this: When motivation begins to wane, take an honest assessment of your effort. Has it also waned? Often it is not our dreams or goals that have withered, but our disciplined effort.

If you are looking for a secret to motivation, this is it: disciplined and continual effort is the key. Continuing on despite setbacks and hardships even – and perhaps especially – when you feel like stopping is the key to motivation.

"A" IS FOR ATTITUDE

Pessimism kills motivation. The doom and gloom of pessimism quickly engulfs any motivation that might have been glimmering. People who are pessimistic can become angry and resentful of others who surpass them, and they are quick to offer excuses as to why they are left behind.

Look around at those you know who are motivated. They are not angry or pessimistic about the things they are doing. Instead, they are passionate and enthusiastic about their lives and optimistic about their goals and dreams. Who has ever achieved great things with a scowl on their face? *A positive and hopeful attitude is a prerequisite for motivation.*

EMPLOYEE MOTIVATION *AND* ENGAGEMENT

Motivation and engagement are connected, but they are not the same thing. You can have a motivated employee who isn't engaged, but it's hard to find an engaged employee who isn't also motivated. The following statements outline, in an elementary way, the difference between a motivated employee and an engaged employee.

Motivated Employee: What's the benefit to me? What do I gain?

Engaged Employee: What's the benefit for our organization (or the people we serve)? Why does my work matter?

Put another way, imagine watching two employees working hard on a project for which they will receive a bonus if the deadline is met. Initially, both employees are equally committed to completing the task on time. Both employees clearly seem motivated. However, as the deadline nears, it becomes apparent that the project will not be completed on time and the bonuses will not be earned. Seeing this, one of the employees puts less effort and energy into the project than before. He is no longer motivated by the bonus and therefore definitely not engaged. The other employee continues on with the same level of engagement she had before it became apparent that the deadline would be missed. She clearly wants to do right by the client and has the best interests of the organization in mind, not just her own.

Employees who are only motivated for personal reasons need rewards in order to do good work. Engaged employees, on the other hand, do good work for the sake of doing good work. As a leader, the choice between the two is clear. I am looking to fill our organization with engaged employees. The by-product of an engaged employee is that you also get a motivated one.

I WAS JUST THINKING

I am always thinking about work – at random hours of the night, at weddings (terrible, I know), and as I'm "listening" to my wife. Name a place or occasion when I'm not supposed to be thinking about work, and I am. It's my nature; my wheels are always turning. Why am I always thinking about work? Because I am motivated and engaged with my work.

I love when employees say things like, "Hey Randy, last night I was just thinking…" or "Hey Randy, an interesting thought occurred to me on my drive in to work this morning…." When I hear staff initiate conversations in this way, it is confirmation that they too are motivated and engaged with their work. They care enough that they are thinking about work in their discretionary time.

Verbal cues of engaged workers include several phrases:

- "I just had an idea."
- "I've found a quicker way to complete this task."
- "I've been wondering if there is a better way to do this project."

Engaged workers can also display nonverbal cues:

- Staying late to get a job completed.
- Cleaning up when they don't have to.
- Volunteering for additional assignments.

The key theme is that engaged employees are committed to and feel a connection to the organization. They know their work is connected to more than some external reward. A paycheck does matter, but it should be the by-product of motivation and engagement, not the source.

Engaged employees demonstrate care and dedication in their work. They are more willing to take on additional responsibilities, and they care about the organization's success. *Engaged employees use discretionary time, brainpower, and effort beyond what is expected.*

THE DISENGAGED
Unfortunately, research shows that most employees are not engaged.

Instead, many view their work as a meaningless, boring means to an end – a paycheck. A large report published by Gallup concluded that a mere 13 percent of workers feel engaged at their place of work. These are the employees who feel a connection to their organization, and they are productive and loyal.

In contrast, 63 percent of workers are "not engaged," meaning that, though they come to work, they have little energy for their work and feel a limited connection to the organization. They do the bare minimum of what is required and invest no discretionary effort.

The remaining 24 percent are "actively disengaged," meaning they are unhappy, unmotivated, and actively looking for ways to do less work. They may even intentionally undermine the efforts of the organization.[1]

This means that close to 90 percent of the people surveyed are working in jobs they don't like, for organizations they are indifferent about at best and loathe at worst. The negative impacts of an unmotivated and disengaged workforce are not likely lost on most leaders. Where there is a lack of engaged employees, low productivity is sure to follow.

ASSESSING ENGAGEMENT

Leaders should not need an assessment tool to inform them of whether their employees are engaged at a fundamental level. If we are honest with ourselves, we more often than not already know. The cues and clues will be there, either indicating engagement or a lack of it. However, surveys and assessments can be helpful for providing clarity into various nuances of engagement. On page 183, in the Resources section, is an example of an employee engagement assessment tool.

Regrettably, poorly thought out employee engagement assessments and surveys are all too common. When organizations introduce assessments in a hurried or confused way, when they don't share the results with employees, and when they offer no concrete plan for change as a result of the assessments, they risk further alienating their employees.

A key consideration when conducting any survey or assessment is that you need to be prepared to manage and attend to the findings. Sharing the results with employees is equally important. This demonstrates respect for employee feedback. If organizations are not prepared to share results and develop action plans based on their findings, they shouldn't even conduct an assessment. What is the point of an assessment if the results aren't used?

On the other hand, when an organization's leadership acts on findings, changes processes, and takes action based on feedback, it concretely demonstrates to employees that they are not just open to hearing about concerns, but they are also committed to responding to them. The positive impact of a well-thought-out assessment process is that it tells employees that you care about engagement.

THE NUMBER ONE CULPRIT

While employees have a responsibility to show up to work motivated and engaged, the onus of fostering and sustaining engagement rests largely on leadership. If leadership is not creating the right environment, a lack of engagement is not the employees' fault.

While building the right environment for engagement requires a multifaceted approach, I believe that the ways in which leaders treat their employees have the strongest impact on employee engagement. An employee's immediate manager has an essential role in building employee engagement. The well-used adage, "Employees don't quit their organization, they quit their direct manager," is especially true when it comes to engagement.

In a 2012 study by Dale Carnegie & Associates, Inc., employees clearly indicated that their personal relationships with their managers were key to engagement. In particular, they wanted "caring" managers. Employees want their managers to take an interest in and care about their lives.[2]

This theme of a caring and compassionate leader also emerged when analyzing the written employee responses to our own survey. Here is an observation from one employee who echoed the insights of many others: "Compassion and empathy are essential because your staff needs to feel like you honestly care and that it is not just lip service."

Leaders who connect with employees by being likable, warm, and empathetic are more likely to have an engaged workforce. On the other hand, leaders who are disconnected, or who devalue or distrust employees, further decrease engagement.

CHARACTERISTICS OF ENGAGEMENT

Another common element found across organizations with engaged workforces is that they provide an array of nonfinancial benefits. These organizations do not view nonfinancial benefits simply as after-thoughts, and neither do their employees. For most employees, at least the ones you want in your organization, these elements are key reasons for engagement.

In workplaces with high levels of employee engagement, you will find that employees

- have a say and participate in planning and decision-making,
- are proud to work for their organization,
- have a sense of control and autonomy in their work,
- believe that their organization makes a difference,
- have the freedom to offer opinions and ideas,
- feel like they belong and are connected to coworkers and leaders,
- have responsibilities and can influence direction for a specific domain or area,
- are challenged and get a strong sense of personal accomplishment and satisfaction from their work, and
- see a connection between their day to day work and the larger purpose of the organization.

● ● ● ● ● ● ● ● ● ● ● ● ● ● ● ●

EMPLOYEE SURVEY RESPONSES

"Autonomy energizes me to work harder, work smarter, and take more creative risks."

"Nothing motivates an employee more than loyalty."

"I want to have the satisfaction of a job well done. I also want the opportunity to grow beyond my job description and expand my horizons."

"I am more motivated when I have done a good job on a task and I am acknowledged accordingly."

● ● ● ● ● ● ● ● ● ● ● ● ● ● ● ●

In workplaces with high levels of employee engagement, you will find that leaders

- keep employees informed about issues impacting the organization,
- make organizational health a key priority,
- let employees decide the "how" when assigning tasks,
- give people the right tools to do their jobs,
- care about employee well-being,
- provide clear vision for the future,
- ask employees to dream and think about the future of the organization,
- ask employees for their opinions before making major decisions that impact them, and
- celebrate employees who experiment with new processes and generate new ideas.

● ● ● ● ● ● ● ● ● ● ● ● ● ● ● ●

LEADER SURVEY RESPONSES

"Avoid secrets. Secrets will kill an organization. They demotivate employees and cause mistrust."

"Staff are more motivated when their opinions are heard and taken seriously."

"Link the work that employees are doing to the big picture."

"A good leader is willing to explain the *why* of a decision so that people can support it and move forward."

● ● ● ● ● ● ● ● ● ● ● ● ● ● ● ●

AUTONOMY, MASTERY, AND PURPOSE

One of the most compelling TED Talks about motivation and engagement is Daniel Pink's "The Puzzle of Motivation." His book, *Drive: The Surprising Truth About What Motivates Us,* is equally insightful.

In his talk and book, Pink reviews three essential elements needed for improving employee motivation and engagement:

1. **Autonomy**: the ability to influence one's own path and direction.
2. **Mastery**: the ability to see progress and get better at something that matters.
3. **Purpose**: the desire to work in an organization that matters and makes a difference in something larger than ourselves.

He believes that "human beings have an innate inner drive to be autonomous, self-determined, and connected to one another. And when that drive is liberated, people achieve more and live richer lives."[3]

WHAT ABOUT MONEY?

Pink argues that once employees are paid enough to cover their essential needs, and assuming this pay is standard across the industry, organizations need to look beyond rewards as a way of motivating and engaging employees. Once financial needs are met, what employees really desire is to be self-directed, to master things, and to be a part of something that's important.

While it is true that engagement must be built and sustained with nonfinancial elements, money also matters. Employees need to make a reasonable amount of money to live comfortably. This particularly matters at the low end of the salary scale where any additional dollar can make a big difference to an individual. It also matters if people perceive that they are being underpaid compared to their colleagues or to other workplaces. Without competitive pay, organizations can't even begin to attract the type of talent that is engaged.

FINANCIAL BONUSES

Not everyone reading this book works in an organization that has the option of providing financial bonuses. If you are fortunate enough to be in an organization that does, there are many things to consider. While bonuses have the potential to motivate, they can also be demotivating if used poorly.

Here are some essential guidelines we have developed:

- Bonuses are clearly on top of basic pay. Reducing pay in order to develop a bonus scheme will likely have a negative impact.
- When our organization does well financially, we want to share some of that success with our employees. In many ways, bonuses are less about motivation and more about thanking our employees for their hard work and engagement.
- Bonuses are given once a year if our organization's financial targets are met. In our case, these targets have been reached about

80 percent of the time, so there is a proven track record of meeting them. I have seen other organizations set unrealistic targets and tell employees about a potential bonus that never arrives. After years of receiving no bonuses, employees become cynical.

We give bonuses based on the following criteria: 10 percent of salary for those with three or more years of service, 7 percent of salary for those with two years of service, and 5 percent of salary for those with one year of service.

The increase in bonuses over time is designed to help employees see that commitment to the organization can have future financial rewards. The size of the bonus is significant because I believe it needs to be large to be effective. We see our bonus plan as one of several things we are doing to sustain engagement.

FINDING MEANING IN THE MUNDANE

The reality is that all of us – employees and leaders alike – have responsibilities that are either mundane or that we simply dislike. It's very hard to be excited about some tasks, yet the everyday, sometimes mundane undertakings are important, and they require as much attention as the tasks we find more meaningful and enjoyable. To discover the focus and attention that is required for these mundane tasks, motivation must be connected to a higher purpose.

Employees want to be part of something bigger than their tasks. Leaders must help employees find a sense of purpose in their work that goes beyond simply completing their everyday responsibilities. Employees will participate and even excel in these less than desirable roles if they believe their work is connected to a greater purpose.

TALENT MOTIVATES TALENT

Motivated and engaged employees want to work with other motivated and engaged people – in fact, they thrive on it.

One of our employees recently indicated that a key reason he chose to join our team was that he would be able to work with other people he viewed as highly talented, motivated, and engaged. It is exciting and energizing to work with great talent. Employees who are motivated and engaged feed off each other for the betterment of the organization.

When you have a team of highly motivated and engaged employees, they not only manage themselves, they manage each other. I have found that an average employee in the presence of exceptional and engaged employees will either raise their level of talent and engagement or they will leave the organization. If the majority of your employees are engaged, they will set the standard for what is expected of new hires. *Talent motivates talent!*

ENGAGEMENT AS VIEWED BY EMPLOYEES

I interviewed some of our staff for this portion of the book and asked them to identify the things that their leaders and organization do to help them be motivated and engaged. These are some of their responses:

- "Our leaders are enthusiastic and motivated, and they love new ideas and change. Motivation and engagement is contagious when it comes from the top."
- "We are not just drones, with leaders making decisions. We are encouraged to be involved, have ideas, and be creative."
- "What we do has value outside our walls. What we do goes into the local and broader community as well. Our work is important and worthwhile."
- "People matter. The people I work with are a large reason why I want to come to work."
- "Whether it's entering data, packing a box, or creating an ad, we understand how that task fits into the purpose of our organization."

- "I'm given autonomy in how I structure my workflow, and I'm given the freedom to think about new ways of doing things."
- "I am able to always learn new things and improve. I'm never told, 'Just do your job.'"
- "I'm not kept in the dark about what's going on in our organization. I'm informed and involved."
- "Our leadership is great at identifying employee strengths and giving us tasks in those areas. Having tasks that I like brings me satisfaction and increases my motivation even more."
- "I see the bigger picture even in my mundane tasks. What we do matters and is important to me."

These statements by our employees reassure me of their engagement. Our employees are satisfied with their work. They view much of the work they do as challenging and interesting. Our employees value the autonomy and discretion they have in how they organize their time. They challenge and stretch themselves to expand their knowledge and expertise, and they continually learn new things. They like who they work with and for, and they appreciate that they engage with good people while at work. Work is more than a job, it is an extension of their lives. Finally, there is an element of meaning to their work. Their work matters and is a part of something bigger than themselves.

ANOTHER LEADER'S INSIGHTS

JEFF SCHMIDT, Dolphin School

Jeff Schmidt is the principal of a small private school. He leads a staff of 50 and a student body of 200 children. Jeff is a leader who works purposefully to motivate and engage his staff.

I know that when I'm working at my best, that's when I feel some sense of motivation with my job. In my career, it has always been important to find what really speaks to my soul. When you do discover those areas that you really thrive in, suddenly you find that your motivation jumps up a level. It's that feeling that you are doing what you were absolutely born to do.

I love seeing my teachers when they are thriving – there's a sense that everyone is moving in rhythm with each other like a finely oiled machine. When I see this, it motivates me as a leader even more.

One of my biggest observations is that when you give staff something that they can really chew on and dig their teeth into, they will fly. To motivate my staff, my approach is to draw on people's strengths. I try to get staff doing what I know they are brilliant at.

I had one staff member who was just floating along. I knew he had a keen interest in technology, so when we needed someone to take the lead on a new computer system we were implementing, I reached out to him. He was so excited about this new role and took it on with gusto. Now, instead of just floating along, he's passionate about what he's doing. He comes in early and stays late. He's coming to me with new ideas. I just see his excitement so much more than ever before.

I've also learned that staff find it motivating when you acknowledge their work. Many of my teachers are pouring their souls into their lessons, and they're putting together amazing plans. They want to be acknowledged for this work that they are doing. Employees need to be told, "You're doing a great job."

What doesn't work to motivate staff is micromanagement. I believe micromanaging is incredibly dangerous because staff feel that they can't step out of line. As a leader, you have to trust people to do their jobs.

I think the idea that *talent motivates talent* is very true. I see it in children on the soccer field. Children don't gravitate toward others who are not as good as they are. They want to play with the big kids. They want to play with the best because they want to be better.

I've always loved working with people who are more talented than I am. When someone has mastered something, you can see it clearly and you are simply drawn to them. We had a guest poet come visit our school. He spoke to our children and staff for 45 minutes. By the end of his presentation, he had all of us eating out of his hand. Every single one of us was ready to write poetry. It was amazing!

When things are running really well, it is natural to want to be a part of it. I think whenever we are around other people who are really passionate and good at what they do, we want to be a part of what they are doing.

I have one group of staff in particular that is extremely engaged and on fire. They are always working together and sharing ideas freely. After school they will meet and talk about how to do things differently, get the most out of the children, or solve a problem with a particular child. When I observe these moments, I see how happy they are and how much they love what they are doing – I see how engaged they are. They love, just love, being a part of their small team and this school.

—Jeff Schmidt

QUESTIONS FOR REFLECTION

1. What signs of motivation and engagement are visible in your organization?
2. Can you identify people in your organization who are motivated but not engaged? What about people who are both motivated and engaged? What differences do you notice between them?
3. Where have you seen disengagement? How has leadership contributed to that disengagement?
4. How does your organization, and how do you as a leader, provide an environment that fosters engagement? Consider the lists under the heading "Characteristics of Engagement" on page 21.

2

PASSION

● ● ● ● ● ● ● ● ● ●

A VOCATION OF PASSION

Many members of my extended family are involved in agriculture. In my youth I worked on my grandfather's and uncle's farms. At the time, I was not able to appreciate the driving force that led so many of my family members to choose farming as a vocation.

It was clear to me from an early age that hard work was one of our core family values. It was expected and applauded, while anything less was unacceptable. At the time, I wasn't able to see that *passion* was actually our family ethos. *Hard work was the result of being passionate about something.*

My brother Joe is one of the most passionate people I know. Though I left the farming community of my youth, my brother continued to work on farms after high school. He slowly started to build his own farm, first by buying a few cows and housing them at my uncle's farm, then by renting a farm and buying some used equipment.

After many years of hard work, Joe was able to purchase his own farm. If you know anything about farming, you will know it is difficult and almost unheard of for someone to start a farm without the help of a parent who is also farming.

I have watched my brother toil relentlessly over the years, working long hours for little income. Farmers quickly learn to never calculate their hourly wages – they know that knowledge would be far too depressing.

I have seen Joe go through periods where any other rational person would have quit, but Joe persevered. Now, 25 years later, he has an established farm. Grieser Dairy Farm not only survived the difficult times, but now thrives as a result of his passion.

Without passion for your work, and without passion for your vision of the future, it is difficult to persevere. It takes more than a strong work ethic to keep going in hard times. Even in the most difficult of times, my brother's passion remained. Farming is what he does, breathes, lives, and loves. His passion for farming is infectious. He can't help but tell you his dreams and visions, as well as the current challenges and struggles on the farm. Passionate people are always looking to share their thoughts and ideas with anyone who will listen.

WHY PASSION MATTERS

Passion is a profound positive feeling for something deeply and personally meaningful that evokes energy, excitement, and enthusiasm.

Passion, as well as a lack of passion, is contagious. No one has ever been inspired by a leader who is not passionate. If you want to have a passionate, inspired workforce, it must begin with you, the leader. Passion inspires others to join and identify with your vision.

Passion elevates productivity and ensures employee commitment to your vision. It is born out of something that is intensely meaningful to you. It is not a general hobby or a fleeting interest; rather, it is core to who you are. Turning vision into reality requires passion.

When you are passionate about something, you can't help but think about it, work at it, and be excited about it. Your passion determines your actions and decisions on a daily basis. Passion eventually leads to mastery and success in large part because you are always thinking about and working on the things you are passionate about. *Most successful leaders don't have a job – they have a passion.*

● ● ● ● ● ● ● ● ● ● ● ● ● ● ● ●

LEADER SURVEY RESPONSES

"Passion is everything, and if you are motivated and driven to be successful, it's usually an indicator that you believe in the work you are doing."

"Love what you do and do what you love – otherwise you're boring."

● ● ● ● ● ● ● ● ● ● ● ● ● ● ● ●

PASSION IS ROOTED IN PURPOSE
A leader's or organization's purpose is not always immediately apparent, but when you look closely, you can usually find that aspiring to make a difference is what drives passion. To make a more useful product or to provide a better service, one must be passionate about making a difference.

In our mission statement at ACHIEVE and CTRI, our focus on making a difference is articulated as a desire to make lives better. Our mission is "to provide exceptional training and resources to better lives."

My proudest moments as the leader of our organization come when I hear from clients how we have somehow helped them, their families, or their own clients. Making a difference matters to me and the senior leaders of our organization, and because it matters to us, it is much easier for our staff to share our passion.

START WITH *WHY*
Simon Sinek's TED Talk "How Great Leaders Inspire Action" and his

book *Start With Why: How Great Leaders Inspire Everyone to Take Action* present a concept he calls "The Golden Circle." He uses it to provide a compelling insight into why some leaders and organizations have more influence than their peers, and it all starts with *why*.

> Very few people or companies can clearly articulate *why* they do *what* they do… By *why* I mean what is your purpose, cause, or belief? *Why* does your company exist? *Why* do you get out of bed every morning? And *why* should anyone care?[1]

Sinek asserts that while most people can usually articulate the *what* and *how* of what they do, it is the *why* that matters most. It is the *why* that leaders need to focus their attention on.

BUILDING PASSION IN EMPLOYEES

Far too many people lack passion for their work. There are employees who feel trapped, are bored, or simply hate their jobs. Because of this, the organizations they work for can only achieve so much. These employees become stuck and are limited by their lack of passion. Without passion, employees will not sustain the energy and focus necessary to help their organizations truly succeed and make a difference.

Having passion as a leader is one thing, but inspiring passion in your employees is another altogether. Employees will not automatically be passionate about the work they do. Perhaps for a short time they will, but if you are aiming for long-term engaged passion, you need to be intentional about providing inspiration.

Leaders inspire employees to be passionate by expressing genuine enthusiasm and articulating why the organization does what it does – why and how the organization makes a difference.

Too often I have worked with organizations whose leaders have a clear idea of how they make a difference, but they have kept this information to themselves. They haven't shared and talked with their staff about why and how the organization makes a difference. Think about it: Do your employees know why your organization exists? Do they know how your organization makes a difference?

Employees expect leaders to be passionate, and if you are not, why would they be? To inspire passion in employees, leaders must be vocal and excited about why the organization matters, and employees need to see and hear that their leaders are passionate about this. In turn, employees will become more passionate.

● ● ● ● ● ● ● ● ● ● ● ● ● ● ●

EMPLOYEE SURVEY RESPONSES

"Who wants to work for someone who doesn't care about the organization they are leading?"

"If leaders have no passion for what they do, why should their employees?"

● ● ● ● ● ● ● ● ● ● ● ● ● ● ●

PASSION FOR A POSITIVE WORK ENVIRONMENT

At ACHIEVE and CTRI, we have always made a difference by providing exceptional training and resources that better our clients' lives. In the early years of our organization, this was our primary focus and passion. However, a subtle change began to occur several years ago when another passion emerged. I have always cared about providing a good work environment, but in the past few years I have gone from caring about it to being passionate about actively creating an exceptional place for people to work.

The reality is that most of us spend almost half of our waking hours at work. This fact alone should be enough impetus for leaders to provide exceptional workplaces. I am passionate about providing a work environment that makes a difference in the lives of those who work with us. I find a great deal of satisfaction in knowing that our staff have a place to earn a living doing great work in an environment that is also caring and supportive.

WARREN BUFFETT AND PASSION

One of my all-time favorite books is Warren Buffett's biography, *Tap Dancing to Work*. Buffett is a man of passion who continues to love what he does. Well into his 80s he keeps doing what he's been doing because of passion, not for money. In fact, Buffett has pledged to give away 99 percent of his wealth either during his life or after his death.

A person committed to giving away his wealth is motivated by more than just financial gain. He could retire any time, and could have done so when he was 40, yet he continues to work with the same level of commitment and focus as he did then. But why would you retire when you are passionate about what you do?

Warren Buffett is one of the few prominent figures I refer to in this book, and most would consider him to be far from *ordinary*. Although I have never met him, people who write about him clearly regard him as a thoughtful leader, and I have come to see him that way too. I believe we can learn from his example. Buffett has mastered his domain of finance and investments and has become successful. He has reached this level of success not just because he has a higher intellect, works harder, or is luckier than the rest of us, but because of his passion for what he does.

Buffett once told students at the University of Nebraska: "If there is any difference between you and me, it may simply be that I get up every day and have a chance to do what I love to do every day."[2]

When people love what they do, mastering and succeeding at that activity is the result, not the purpose. Success comes as a by-product of the passion. One should not concentrate on success or profit, but on passion. Rewards and success will come, or not come. It is the passion that matters and makes a difference.

IT'S FINALLY FRIDAY

I grew up listening to the country greats: Johnny Cash, Willie Nelson, and George Jones to name a few. For a certain period, several times each Friday, I heard George Jones belt out, "It's finally Friday, I'm free again." The music industry boasts no shortage of songs about the joys of Fridays and the drudgery of Mondays. Their message: work is something to avoid at all costs and to celebrate when done.

I'm not sure I "tap dance" to work every day like Warren Buffett, but I'm usually pretty keen to get to work – especially in the morning. I make sure I get to bed early enough so I can enjoy the morning. It's when I'm most excited, happy, and motivated, and it's when I get my best work done.

When you are passionate about your work, you wake up excited about the day ahead. You just can't wait to get the day started. I don't think of work as some negative part of life to be endured until Friday, then set aside and resented come Monday.

LIFE, NOT WORK-LIFE

I have personally struggled for years with the concept of a work-life balance. Even the combination of words troubles me. The hyphen between the words "work" and "life" irritates me because the wordsmiths are trying to have it both ways.

By separating the words "work" and "life," we are meant to see them as two distinct parts. Yet that is actually a myth, for *work is a part of life*. So the hyphen is inserted as a reminder that the two can't actually be separated. Wouldn't it all be simpler if we just used one word: *life*?

I believe in *life* balance. My passions include work, family, friends, travel, and fitness (namely mountain biking). This is my life in a nutshell. When you meet me, you will usually see me engaged in, talking about, or thinking about one of these five aspects of my life. I don't talk too much about religion, politics, or the arts, for they are not my passions – and please don't ask me to go to the ballet or opera.

Work is not separated out from my other passions. I don't have one category for work and another for family, friends, travel, and fitness. I can be just as passionate about a new product at work as I am about eating at that great restaurant with my family in France, the one where I clearly remember the tastes, the music, and the conversation. I am as excited about securing a new client at work as I am about trying out my new mountain bike.

There are many different components to my life, but it is all *life* nonetheless. The "work-life" advocates try to guilt me into separating and compartmentalizing my life, but I resist. Work is life-giving in the same way my family and friends are life-giving. I talk about work with my family and friends, and I talk about my family and friends with my colleagues at work. My passions are interconnected – not separate.

THE PROBLEM WITH UNBALANCED PASSION

By no means should you think I am advocating for a regular 80-hour work week. Nor am I proposing that your work should be your only passion. If the only passion in your life is work, you are probably missing out on a great deal that life has to offer, and it will not be sustainable in the long term.

I know people, including myself, who work long hours and focus an enormous amount of energy on work-related activities, but who also have other passions that sustain them. Unfortunately, I also know people who work just as long and hard but have no other passions. They can live this way for a time and seem okay, but eventually most will either burn out or become miserable.

I believe that having interests and passions other than work actually helps me at work. I am a more balanced person because of my different passions. Work alone is not enough to sustain a person.

GLIMPSES OF PASSION

Look around you, and while you will see people and organizations that lack passion, you will also see many that do have passion. I have already shared with you how my brother lives life with passion. I also see it at my children's school. I see teachers do amazing things. They creatively educate my children because they are passionate about the work they do. This kind of engagement in work is not possible without passion.

The social services field also stands out to me for the number of people who passionately do their work. I often do work in this field through our training and consulting practices, and I always walk away from these experiences humbled and inspired by the passion these workers and organizations have. These individuals are working from and for a sense of purpose. They are driven by their desire to make a difference, and this comes from their passion.

Passionate leaders and employees are out there everywhere, often in small organizations doing unique and creative things. These organizations have leaders who aren't bystanders – they are actively involved and engaged with their employees, and they work to mobilize their organizations in a common direction for a common cause. They believe that what they do makes a difference! They have passion.

ANOTHER LEADER'S INSIGHTS

PETE LOEWEN, Country Cycle

Pete owns and operates a small bike shop as well as its cycling club and race team. He employs two other bike enthusiasts. Pete is a passionate leader who inspires others to join his passion for biking.

I just went for a long, amazing bike ride this morning, and then I stopped for a cappuccino. How awesome is that?

Biking is just such a great motivator. You realize after a bike ride how good it makes you feel. Biking always brings me back to the simplicity of life. It's play. It makes me feel like a kid again. It's a simple joy, and I want to share that with other people. That's the root of my passion for biking – I want people to feel what I'm feeling when I'm on a bike. Yes, I'm passionate about biking, but I'm just as passionate about creating a community.

One of the key things I focus on in our bike club is being inclusive. We want anybody who wants to get into biking to feel welcome, regardless of what their background is or what kind of shape they are in. We have people in our bike club who used to be unhealthy – smoking, overweight, and inactive. Once they found biking, all of a sudden they had a healthy outlet.

My employees are just as obsessive about biking as I am. When a customer comes in to look for a bike, I want my employees to get excited. Obviously, if you are enthusiastic about bikes, a potential customer is much more likely to get excited too.

I've learned the hard way that hiring people who don't share that same passion for biking is a waste of time. When those employees talked to customers there was just no electricity. I need employees working here who are excited about bikes.

It was tough building this place. Those first few years of business were intense, and I think if I wouldn't have had a passion for it, I would have shut the doors. Having passion for what I was doing is what made me want to stick with it. I kept at it, and I was actually able to realize the kind of vision I had when I started Country Cycle. Passion kept me going through the hard times.

The nice thing is that I still have lots of ideas for what more to do. I don't think I'll ever really retire. Even once I have the ability to slow down, I will still be very invested in improving what we've created.

I definitely don't see what I do as a job. I see it all as life. I love – just love – what I'm doing. I've had jobs where the buzzer rings and you run out the door as fast as you can. Not anymore. Now there isn't really a distinction between work and life – it melds together as one.

—*Pete Loewen*

QUESTIONS FOR REFLECTION

1. In both your personal and professional life, what are you truly passionate about?
2. How does your organization make a difference?
3. Where do you see passionate leaders and employees in your life? What are they like to be around?
4. How effective are you at promoting passion in those around you? What could you do to be more effective?

3

VISION

●●●●●●●●●●

THE FUTURE

My thinking has always been future oriented. In grade nine I was already looking ahead to college. By the time I made it to college, I was ready to move on from there too – I was eager to work. Many of my friends took time to travel during these years, but not me! I had "important" things to do, and that required me to stick to a plan. Time was of the essence. The future was coming, and I was going to be ready for it.

Shortly after starting my first job, I realized that more education would help me reach my future goals. So I went back to school to obtain another degree. I worked again for a few years, moving between jobs and trying to find the right fit. I was always reaching for something bigger and better – something still out there to be achieved. Graduate school was next. I was older now and still not where I had envisioned I should be, so I pushed on with a greater sense of urgency.

Finished with school, I could finally find a job where I would be content, or so I thought. Two years into a new job, that old familiar feeling came back – that sense of being unsettled and needing more. I began to dream and ponder: *What's next?* Shortly thereafter I moved to a new city, excited about a new opportunity.

A few weeks into my new job, I found that I still wasn't satisfied. Why couldn't I be happy and content like so many others? This time, instead of moving on, I began creating a workshop so that I could offer training in addition to my regular work. I hoped this would resolve my angst and need for something more. And it did, for this was the start of CTRI and ACHIEVE.

Before my current role, the longest I had ever held a job was three years. That was the most I could handle before the feeling of needing more would overtake me. My vision for the future was always brighter than the present. There was always something more, bigger, and better out there. I still feel that way. You won't see me leaving for a new job, but that doesn't mean I'm settled.

There is more to do. More to accomplish and explore. My vision for the future of ACHIEVE and CTRI is far greater than their current state. So I continue – always striving for more, always looking toward the future.

VISIONARY LEADERS

Vision is our view of the future. Vision is the portrait of our hopes and dreams. It is our mental picture of what might be, but is not yet. Vision gives us a sense of purpose and guides us as we work in the present. In organizations, a vision statement articulates what the organization aspires to accomplish.

Visionary leaders energize and inspire people to work toward this future goal. They are able to clearly and vividly communicate what the future holds. Visionary leaders anticipate what's coming, both opportunities and obstacles. They are able to connect the dots between various trends and events and interpret how what is happening today might impact the future.

Visionary leaders work with the end in mind. They know where they are headed and why they are going there. They are able to work in the present moment while also looking forward to where the organization is heading. They provide strong direction for the path ahead and give well-defined rationale for how the decisions of the present relate to the vision of the future.

There are very few examples of leaders who have achieved success without a crystal-clear focus on their target. Therefore, it is difficult for a leader to delegate the task of visioning. This process needs to be filled primarily by the leadership of an organization. Leaders can be helped by others in the organization, but leadership ultimately provides guidance for what the future will hold.

SEEING THINGS EARLY

Visionary leaders see things and make sense of them before most others are able to. We do not merely see the obvious opportunities, obstacles, or indicators of change, we also see the subtle trends and discrete events that only a watchful eye can locate – things that appear disconnected and are often found on the periphery of our normal focus.

Not only are visionary leaders able to see things early, we are also able to put various pieces of information together in a manner that is coherent and makes sense. Despite being bombarded with information from multiple sources, we are able to filter through what is important and what is not. We are able to put seemingly random pieces of information together and draw logical and meaningful conclusions from them.

To see things early, I regularly step back from my day-to-day work and consider the larger world I am living in. Challenging assumptions and asking difficult questions are regular parts of how I gain a clear view.

I am always scanning the wider landscape, looking for things that may impact our organization either positively or negatively. I have learned that it is important to be able to zoom in and focus on meaningful details and then step back and see how those details relate to other areas. The challenge is to be able to filter out the cluttered noise that surrounds us so we can focus in on what is relevant.

● ● ● ● ● ● ● ● ● ● ● ● ● ● ● ●
LEADER SURVEY RESPONSES

"In leadership you need the ability to predict, analyze, and prepare for potential hazards or roadblocks that might prevent you from achieving the vision."

"Without vision, you don't have much."

"Leaders must be able to effectively identify what needs to be done and where they want to go, and then communicate it."

● ● ● ● ● ● ● ● ● ● ● ● ● ● ● ●

VISIONARY LEADERS TAKE RISKS
Visionary leaders use the information we gather to take calculated risks. The information we glean provides insights about the future that others often miss, and this information usually requires us to act quickly in order to benefit from it. Once relevant information is known, doing nothing is rarely an option for visionary leaders.

The degree of risk we face varies from decision to decision. Some risks are potentially costlier, and some risks are more difficult to manage. Yet risk is a part of our lives, and while we can work to mitigate risks, they are still a reality. Even doing nothing is a risk. In fact, the risk of doing nothing may eventually be greater than the risk of taking action.

I have always believed that if we are complacent as an organization, we are at a greater risk of becoming irrelevant. This fear causes me to continually question the way things are and to push our organization to explore new opportunities. *There must be progress – there must be more – and progress always requires a certain level of risk.*

SEEING THINGS THAT IMPACT YOUR FUTURE

When envisioning the future, it is essential to understand the factors that will impact the world, many of which will also impact your organization. As we make decisions about the future, we should do so with as much information as possible. While we cannot predict the future, there are indicators and trends that can lead us to meaningful conclusions if we pay attention.

In our organization, when we ponder what our future might look like, we do so with an eye on the following five key domains:

1. **Economy**: How will the local, national, and international economies impact our organization? What is the current economic situation, and what do the experts project?
2. **Politics**: How will the current and projected government impact our organization? How stable is the existing government? What governmental policies may impact our organization?
3. **Demographics**: How will changing demographics, such as an aging population or increased immigration, affect our organization? How do these changes impact how we deliver our services and products?
4. **Technology**: How will new technologies change our organization? What do we need to do now to prepare for projected changes in technology?
5. **Competition**: How will our competition impact our success? What are they doing that we are not? What strengths do they have that we can learn from?

Visioning for the future must take these external influences into account. Changes in these five areas can fundamentally shift the viability of your organization as it is currently structured. Visioning without taking these variables into consideration creates an undue level of risk and vulnerability. Yet the very nature of variables is that they will change. Therefore visioning for the future is not a one-time exercise, but an ongoing one.

It is easy to identify opportunities or obstacles in retrospect, but that is often too late to take advantage of them or avoid possible disasters. When we are not ahead of an opportunity, we are simply joining a fad whose time has already passed. Worse yet, when we are not seeing an obstacle or working to overcome it, our organization can be negatively affected.

Grasping the complexities of these influences requires us to be vigilant, to listen, and to pay attention. I frequently read trade magazines and blogs. I listen to the news – even if the stories don't interest me, I sometimes find information that is relevant or useful. I have found it helpful to step outside my comfort zone and read a random publication. For example, when I fly, I always read through the airline publication, scanning for anything that might prompt a fresh insight.

I see these exercises as a regular part of my workday. One of my roles is to always pay attention and be on the lookout for news, trends, and information that may impact the organization's current and future success.

CHANGING VISIONS

A vision needs to be flexible enough to accommodate new circumstances that will present themselves. New information will inevitably change my vision for the future.

The vision for my organization is rarely static. It may be fixed for a couple of years at most, but then through the process of gathering and evaluating new information, our vision changes. It changes even more when I test the new information and ideas with others in our organization. Our vision for the future really is a moving target. Leaders need to become comfortable with this – *we don't get to settle; we never fully arrive.*

While our vision continually evolves, our mission and purpose – the *why* of what we do – stays fairly static. It's the future that changes and becomes unclear, not our *why*. Yet when our vision for the future changes, it is almost always met with excitement, for it is usually far bolder and more ambitious than the previous vision.

I view our mission, beliefs, and core values as carved in stone, but our vision is pliable clay that never hardens – it can always be molded and shaped.

COMMUNICATE YOUR VISION

Organizations need a vision, but they also need leaders who communicate that vision. Employees look to their leaders to provide an image of the future. Leaders who can clearly articulate their vision inspire others to join them on the journey. The more excited you are about where you're going, the more likely others are to join you.

Sharing your vision, and being receptive to other people's suggestions for that vision, builds a common purpose. It helps people see the bigger picture of why they are working – it motivates them. Leaders who can articulate a compelling vision for the future that connects with people will inspire them to join in working toward that vision.

I have not always been intentional enough about communicating our vision. In recent years, I have been more deliberate about this, and I have quickly seen the benefits. Now, whenever possible, I share our organization's vision with employees. In addition to telling them what I'm thinking, I also listen to their feedback. I have found that the more I talk with others, the clearer our vision for the future becomes.

Very few large-scale visions have ever been achieved without the help of others. As a result of this realization, I have learned that it is important to ask employees to share their thoughts and offer suggestions for the vision of the organization. The insights they have offered have altered our organization's vision in many positive ways. By including others in our thinking and planning for the future, we have created a shared and inclusive future – one that everyone in our organization can feel proud of.

● ● ● ● ● ● ● ● ● ● ● ● ● ● ● ● ●

EMPLOYEE SURVEY RESPONSES

"It is important that employees are included in shaping a vision so that their input and ownership are embedded in the future of the organization."

"It is crucial that leaders are able to identify a clear vision for the future and translate that vision into what it means for me as an employee."

● ● ● ● ● ● ● ● ● ● ● ● ● ● ● ●

MAKING VISION A REALITY

Nothing happens before it is envisioned in someone's mind, but bringing that vision into reality requires more than just a mental picture of what might be. A theme throughout this book is the importance of *doing* the work that is required to achieve success. In this regard, a combination of vision and productivity is essential to reach a future desired place.

I meet far too many people who have amazing visions, but who are not working toward achieving them. Their plans for the future are remarkable, and would often be realistic and doable if only they were working toward achieving their vision. Yet far too few people ever start, let alone finish.

Visions are nice to have – they look and sound good – but seeing them develop to fruition requires a tenacious, sustained drive. This drive is what separates those who see their vision become reality from those who wait for the right time to start, or hope things will magically happen, without putting in the work required. *A vision is meaningless if support isn't given to make it a reality.*

USING STRATEGY TO ACHIEVE VISION

The literature on leadership and management is full of words that have various interpretations. At ACHIEVE and CTRI, we describe the following key words in this way:

- **Mission**: Why we exist.
- **Beliefs**: What gives us purpose.
- **Core Values**: What guides us.
- **Vision**: What we want to be.
- **Strategy**: How we get there.

For more information about our mission, beliefs, vision, and core values, see page 188 in the Resources section of this book. Core values will also be reviewed in more detail in Chapter 5, Talent and Team Selection.

Strategy is the specific plan and set of procedures required to get our day-to-day work done while also attaining our future goals. Strategy helps us determine the practices that will be necessary to bring about and sustain our growth and manage future changes. Strategy helps us both react to the current environment and plan for the future. It is what's required to turn our vision into reality.

Even though I will often use just the term strategy, it can be broken down into strategic thinking and strategic planning. *Strategic thinking* allows us to identify opportunities and challenges, while *strategic planning* helps us take advantage of those opportunities and manage those challenges. Strategic planning requires specificity and detail to create clearly defined steps and objectives.

In many ways, strategy is more tangible and less abstract than vision. We see and use strategy up close almost every single day. In contrast, vision is somewhere *out there*, something not yet present.

STRATEGY IN ACTION

Strategy is what helps us get from here to there. Once we have clearly communicated a vision, everyday strategic decisions can be more easily made with that vision in mind. To achieve our vision, we must have a link from the present to the future. What we do today must be done with the future in mind. I am always aware of the need to balance the tasks and issues of today while keeping my focus on the future.

In my role as a leader, I am ever mindful of workflow and demands: Who is doing what? Whose role is changing? How will this impact staffing needs? Are we ready for the busy season? Do we have projects for the slow season? Do we have the resources and talent for what's next?

To manage these questions, I have one eye on today and another looking six months, a year, and even five years down the road. For me, thinking that far ahead is not really about the future, it is about right now. The decisions we make today will impact our workflow, income, expenses, and staffing needs a year from now. Likewise, the decisions we are making about next year are going to impact our current workflow and tasks.

The importance of this ability cannot be understated: *We must work in the present with a focus on the future, and simultaneously make decisions about the future while making sense of how they impact the present.* I believe that my focus on this balance is a significant factor in our organization's success.

OUR VISION

At ACHIEVE, we envision a future where everyone has access to *high-quality* leadership and workplace development resources. At CTRI, we envision a future where everyone has access to *high-quality* mental health, counseling, and violence-prevention resources. We aspire to be the most *trusted, accessible,* and *widely known* provider of these resources.

The emphases on *high quality, trusted, accessible, and widely known* are the four key pillars of our strategy. Our discussions and plans for the future are centered on these four areas. We continually ask ourselves questions such as:

- What do we need to do to increase the *quality* of our products and services?
- How can we become more *trusted*?
- What can we do to make our training and resources more *accessible* to people?
- How can we expand our market and become more *widely known*?

My key point is that our vision informs and drives our strategy. Our vision has helped us identify very specific and intentional areas in which to focus our strategy. These are areas we believe we need to concentrate on in order to attain our vision.

It is also important to note that we are not yet there. The quality of our products and services can improve, we can be more trusted, our products need to be more accessible, and there are still people to reach with our message. *Our vision is not yet realized. Our vision is not who we are, it is what we want to be.*

BE A VISIONARY LEADER

When organizations lack vision, they are rarely able to thrive. Many organizations struggle because they do not look into the future and see what might be. Rather, they are stuck in keeping up with the present. They lack vision and are unable to prepare for opportunities or obstacles.

People expect their leaders to know where they are going. Our employees expect us to have a vision for the future that gives them hope and inspires them. Providing hope and inspiration requires us to share, with genuine excitement, the possibilities for the future.

As visionary leaders, we must know where we are going, communicate where we are going, and motivate others to join us on that journey.

ANOTHER LEADER'S INSIGHTS

CATHERINE BARGEN, Province of British Columbia
Catherine is the restorative justice coordinator housed within the Ministry of Public Safety and Solicitor General in the province of British Columbia. She is a well-known speaker and leader in the field of restorative justice. Catherine is passionate about her field of practice and identifies clearly with a vision that guides her work.

Vision is important to articulate because without it you really can't motivate others to come along with you. When you actually take time to name a vision, you get much further because you can measure yourself against it. It also helps others understand to what extent they are or aren't on board with your vision.

My vision is to help make restorative justice an accessible, viable, and desirable option for victims. This vision helps shape the choices I make and determines where I put my energy. How are we doing with training? How are we doing with standards? How are we doing with making resources available? Vision really helps direct all kinds of projects I'm involved with.

My vision for restorative justice is not about coming from up above and handing it down. It's more about working away at a grassroots level. I'm not a CEO – I'm not at the front of a ship saying, "Go this way." But I am someone who gets to help influence and lay down strategies for the future.

Part of my vision is to bring key stakeholders together and make sure we are having a dialogue. Sometimes I find myself at the front of a room articulating my vision for restorative justice. I tell people that we are here because we want to advance the practice of restorative justice to be victim sensitive and victim centered.

I love the field of restorative justice, and I love building relationships. I feel invested because my work reflects my own values. Work turns into play for me, and I believe that's what makes me an effective leader. I am interested in restorative justice, I care about how it's done, and I care about how we get there.

The strongest leaders and mentors I have known have had a rock-solid compass on good ethics. They are relationship based, curious, humble listeners, and responsive. They also have a willingness to step aside when their own agendas are getting in the way.

These people I have been inspired by are able to articulate a vision, but they are also able to laugh over a drink and build relationships. I have realized that if you're not building good relationships along the way so that others are using their own investment, talent, and energy to drive the vision, then your vision is not going to go anywhere. You're going to knock your head trying to make things happen.

At the end of accomplishing something satisfying, I want people to say, "We did this!" instead of pointing toward someone else and saying, "You did this!" I want people to say, "We were along, and we're so happy to be a part of the vision."

—*Catherine Bargen*

QUESTIONS FOR REFLECTION

1. How will economy, politics, demographics, technology, and competition impact your organization in the future?
2. What risks have you taken to work toward your future vision?
3. In what ways do you communicate your vision for the future?
4. What strategies have you put in place to achieve your vision?

4

SELF-AWARENESS

●●●●●●●●●●

THE CONFIDENT LEADER

In my youth, some people perceived me as arrogant. I would often reply to these perceptions by saying something like, "I'm not arrogant, I'm just confident and you're jealous."

Of course this came across as an arrogant statement (particularly the "you're jealous" part), and it usually did little to dispel the perception that I was arrogant. Through self-awareness and growth, I have since softened the side of me that others perceived as arrogant.

While arrogance is a negative trait, we do need confidence as leaders. Leaders need to show a certain level of self-assurance. *Employees do not want to follow an insecure leader.*

People follow leaders who are sure of themselves because a leader's confidence assures them they are moving in the right direction and have the support needed to be successful. Confidence is a strength, but it risks becoming a weakness if it blinds a leader to his or her shortcomings.

While I believe my confidence is a strength, I also need to make sure it doesn't prevent me from seeing situations clearly and accurately. It may lead to a lack of listening or an over-reliance on myself, even when others are well positioned to help. I have come to realize that extreme confidence bordering on arrogance is a slippery slope.

MINDFUL LEADERSHIP

Mindfulness is the state of being conscious of the present reality and the practice of becoming aware of one's thoughts and emotions. Those who know me well would say that mindfulness is not a quality often attributed to me. I am more prone to doing, moving, and going – usually at a fast pace. Yet I have my moments of mindfulness too.

While I don't formally "practice" mindfulness, I do find that I'm very aware of and focused on my thoughts, emotions, strengths, and weaknesses. I am particularly given to self-awareness and self-reflection when I am in nature.

Fittingly, I wrote this chapter in Canmore, Alberta, Canada, where I was surrounded by snow-capped mountain peaks. As I wrote, I was able to look out my window and find myself in an awe-inspiring part of the world. I couldn't help but be more reflective than I usually am.

The process of writing this book has been an exercise in self-awareness. The practice of reflecting on and writing about these leadership insights has required me to carefully assess both my strengths and weaknesses. I am particularly mindful of a need to be honest about my limitations.

SELF-AWARENESS MATTERS

Taking the time to be self-aware, to really consider one's strengths and weaknesses, is not something most leaders do very often. They are usually too busy focusing on the seemingly more urgent tasks of any given day to take time for self-reflection.

Developing and practicing self-awareness may not get the attention it warrants, yet it is one of the most important things leaders can do to raise the performance of both themselves and their organizations.

Developing awareness allows us to more clearly and vitally focus on building our strengths while intentionally mitigating and managing our weaknesses. Effective leaders must know and understand themselves. Thankfully, like many things, we can get better at self-awareness over time.

● ● ● ● ● ● ● ● ● ● ● ● ● ● ● ●

LEADER SURVEY RESPONSES

"Leadership is an evolving process that relies on your understanding of yourself (your own strengths and challenges), how you apply that understanding to your daily life, and how willing you are to push your own boundaries."

"You have to know how you are being perceived."

"When I need help, I need to be able to ask for it, and self-awareness allows me to be honest with my employees and do this."

● ● ● ● ● ● ● ● ● ● ● ● ● ● ●

RELATIONAL AND OPERATIONAL DOMAINS

We consistently perform at a high level in our areas of strength. Typically, we also gain satisfaction from our work in those areas. Our weaknesses, however, are those things we are not good at and typically don't enjoy doing.

When I talk about strengths and weaknesses, I distinguish between two different domains: relational and operational. The *relational* domain has to do with how employees experience us as leaders on an interpersonal level. Relational strengths and weaknesses are reflected in how we interact with our peers and those we manage. This includes how we demonstrate skills like respect, empathy, listening, communication, and supportiveness.

I have found that when people talk about the strengths and weaknesses of their leaders, they are most often referring to these relational skills and shortcomings. However, it is also important to focus on the second domain: *operational* skills and abilities. This second domain reflects how competent we are in the practical aspects of managing our organizations. These are the areas related to things such as strategic planning, finance, human resources, and marketing.

To demonstrate how one might focus on self-awareness, I share with you some of my own strengths and weaknesses in these two domains.

MY RELATIONAL STRENGTHS

Over the years I have worked to develop and refine my relational strengths:

- I am direct with feedback. You will know where you stand with me and will not be left wondering what I think. Issues or concerns do not get filed away only to be pulled out and reviewed at an annual performance evaluation. If I have an issue, you will know about it.
- I am available. My door is almost always open. I don't begrudge it when you knock on my door and I hear "Do you have a minute?" I realize that, for you to do your best work, you will sometimes need my input, feedback, or direction, and so I need to be available.
- I am encouraging. Maybe not in a warm and fuzzy way, but you will feel my encouragement in subtle and indirect ways. For example, I will encourage you to take on new projects and give you autonomy to excel in those areas you care about.
- I am thoughtful. I try to put myself in your shoes and treat you how I would want to be treated as an employee.

- I am generous. I give you flexibility, above-average time off, a good wage, and regular wage increases. When possible, I give additional perks like bonuses, meals, and gifts.

MY RELATIONAL WEAKNESSES

Over the years I have also become aware of many of my weaknesses that can get in the way of leading effectively:

- I am very impatient. I get frustrated and upset when you are slow with your work or don't deliver on time.
- I give limited affirmation. My way of thinking is that if you are not getting direct feedback (see strengths), you should assume I'm affirming you – no news is good news.
- I am direct with feedback. That's not a typo. Yes, I identified it as a strength as well, which it can be. But it can also be a weakness, as directness can sometimes come across as insensitive or harsh.
- I react quickly. When I am stressed or hear difficult news, I can become rather short, upset, and sometimes angry.
- I have a tendency to micromanage. I like to be in the know and have my fingers on all aspects of the organization. While this helps me lead operationally, it can be perceived as meddling and taking away autonomy.
- I *do not* do special events well. I am indifferent about the whole birthday thing. I have no clue when your birthday is and don't know the exact date you started working with us.

MY OPERATIONAL STRENGTHS

I have many operational strengths. Like most entrepreneurs, I didn't achieve success by being good at just one thing. I am good at strategic thinking, product design, customer service, and innovation. However, what I'm great at, what I excel at, is marketing. I know marketing is my main operational strength because I think about it all the time. I never tire of it. I anticipate the next time I get to focus on marketing and implement my most recent ideas.

Many leaders I know place marketing and branding at the bottom of their to-do lists. For me, it's always been at the top. Yes, product design and customer service are important, but marketing is where my passion lies.

I sometimes attend marketing conferences to keep me on top of what's happening in the industry. Attendees are typically surprised when they learn I am the CEO of our organization. In many ways I am first a CMO (chief marketing officer), and second a CEO.

MY OPERATIONAL WEAKNESSES

I am not great at human resources or finance, but I can get by and do okay in those areas. Where I really lack interest and capacity is in the area of networking. This surprises many people. Countering my intense focus and passion for marketing, I avoid networking as much as possible.

This is a major weakness for a leader to have, especially in the training industry. To have the CEO of a training company actively avoid networking opportunities is almost unheard of. I am sure I have missed opportunities to grow our business because of my distaste for networking. Yet as much as I know this, I can't bring myself to work on improving this weakness.

I do have extroverted tendencies, and I do appreciate meeting new people in natural contexts or when they already know who I am. But the idea of up-selling myself and my organization in person to people I don't know is just not natural for me.

STRENGTH IN VULNERABILITY

The process of naming one's own weaknesses is an act of strength. People respect leaders who recognize that they are not perfect. They respect the honesty and courage it takes to admit weakness, particularly because so many leaders do not have the strength of character required for honest self-assessment. Even rarer is the leader who articulates these weaknesses.

By showing vulnerability, leaders establish trust and show that they are approachable and human. The act of showing vulnerability works to build solidarity between leaders and staff. Being honest about our weaknesses also helps us understand what we need most from those who work with us.

When leaders act as though they are perfect at everything, they risk alienating their staff. This lack of self-awareness can be extremely costly to a leader. *Nothing undermines your effectiveness as a leader faster than failing to admit mistakes and refusing to show you have weaknesses.*

A leader emphasizing his or her own perfection has the potential to show staff that they are not needed, that the leader can take care of everything. But leaders are human. We are not perfect. We say and do things that we shouldn't. When we fail to admit this, others won't respect or follow us as leaders.

● ● ● ● ● ● ● ● ● ● ● ● ● ● ● ●

EMPLOYEE SURVEY RESPONSES

"I need a leader who is not afraid to inquire – to become more informed when they are delving into an area they know little about. I do not need a leader who pretends to know everything."

"Leaders need to be able to recognize their own strengths and limitations as well as those of their staff."

"Leaders who know of their weaknesses become better when they consult with employees who have valuable experience and knowledge."

● ● ● ● ● ● ● ● ● ● ● ● ● ● ● ●

FINDING STRENGTHS AND WEAKNESSES

The observations I have made about my strengths and weakness are not based on a computer program or a 360-degree assessment tool. Rather, they have been made through good old honest self-reflection, personal assessment, and listening to what I have been told by others over the years.

Some will argue that people can't accurately perceive their own weaknesses and strengths. While I have met people who are completely unaware of themselves, I would argue that if we have to rely solely on an assessment tool or survey to arrive at conclusions about ourselves, our ability to improve on strengths and manage and mitigate weaknesses will be limited. Assessment tools are supplements that can support self-awareness, not replacements for the process of self-reflection.

This is not to say that assessments can't be helpful when used appropriately. In fact, I have taken various assessments, which have served to confirm my own view of myself. I have even learned some additional things about myself. However, it is in the moments of quiet personal reflection that my most profound and key insights have emerged.

Before taking a formalized assessment, try this first: Intentionally schedule some time to reflect. Mark the time in your calendar and put it on your to-do list. When the time comes, go to a quiet place with a pad of paper and a pen (not the computer; remember we are doing this the old fashioned way) and begin jotting down your thoughts. First, focus on your relational strengths and weaknesses, then on your operational strengths and weaknesses. If you need some help to get you going, consider some of the questions in the Leadership Strengths and Weaknesses Assessment located in Resources, page 191.

FOCUS ON BOTH STRENGTHS AND WEAKNESSES

While the ability and desire to recognize one's strengths and weaknesses is crucial, what we do with that knowledge is perhaps even more important. In recent years, there has been a strong push from various books to focus on improving strengths while not worrying as much about weaknesses.

The key premise of this belief is that each person's greatest potential for growth lies in the areas of their greatest strengths. Thus, if a leader is focusing too much energy on improving weaknesses, he or she is taking time away from working on strengths. Most people would agree that mitigating weaknesses is harder than building on the strengths one already has.

While I believe the emphasis on strengths-based leadership has merits, especially in the operational domain, focusing only on strengths in the relational domain has its limitations. *Relational weaknesses have the potential to be so detrimental – and potentially fatal – to the leader that simply managing around them will not suffice.* Sometimes it is imperative to work on and improve areas of weakness. I firmly believe that with the right motivation, weaknesses can and should be improved.

MITIGATING WEAKNESSES

Once relational weaknesses are identified, the next step is to reflect on the impact they may have on people you work with. Great leaders care about the people they work with and would never intentionally hurt their feelings or emotionally harm them. If one's relational weaknesses cause a negative impact for oneself or others, that should provide motivation to work at mitigating them.

Notice I didn't say fix or remove the weakness. In reality, often the best we can hope for is to mitigate the impact of these weaknesses. The difficulty of fixing relational weaknesses is that they are primarily a result of personality. Personalities are very difficult – and many would even say impossible – to change.

I have worked hard to soften my reactions when I am feeling stressed or impatient. I have intentionally worked to provide feedback in a way that does not come across as harsh.

Giving affirmation will likely never be a strength of mine, but I have become more affirming, and not in a way that is disingenuous, where I just check it off my list of things to do. In my own way, I purposely offer sincere affirmation much more often than I used to.

I have worked deliberately to not micromanage all aspects of our organization. I remind myself that I have skilled and competent staff who care about doing quality work, and I am confident in their abilities. I still like to know what is going on, but I give less direction in areas where I used to assert more influence.

While I still don't do the birthday thing, I at least participate – and of course I do eat the treats others provide.

I don't simply manage away my relational weaknesses. I name them, I take ownership of them, and I work on them. However, I also manage around them to a certain extent. I have intentionally hired others whose relational strengths are my relational weaknesses. While this is not an excuse or a reason for me to ignore my weaknesses, it is helpful to have a balancing presence to counter them.

To help me with my operational weakness in human resources, I have hired a leader who excels at managing people issues, an area in which I don't excel.

In terms of networking, I have hired someone who is exceptional at it. We now have a more visible leader engaging, meeting, and networking with potential and existing clients.

To deal with my weakness in the area of finances, I maintain a strong working relationship with my accountants and intentionally work to stay on top of things.

These examples demonstrate that while I am a well-rounded and skilled leader, it is my team that provides the depth needed to compensate for my weaknesses.

BLIND SPOTS

In spite of our best efforts to self-assess both informally and perhaps even formally, we may still have blind spots – weaknesses of which we are unaware. Blind spots may also be weaknesses of which we are aware, but the negative impacts are minimized.

It's hard to mitigate a weakness if you don't know it exists or deny its existence. Blind spot weaknesses tend to be more damaging than known weaknesses because you are not working at mitigating or managing them. *Knowing what you don't know is the first step in addressing your weaknesses.*

Exposing your blind spots will likely take a little more focus and effort. Two ways to do this are assessing mistakes and soliciting feedback from others.

Recurring or significant mistakes can often be an indicator of blind spots. One way to identify blind spots is to think about times people have given you feedback that surprised you or caused you to feel defensive. Spend some time analyzing these mistakes:

- What was your role in the causes of the mistakes?
- What are the patterns or common elements of different mistakes?
- What blind spots do these patterns suggest?

Those who surround you – your friends, family, and coworkers – often know things about you that you don't know yourself. Ask them for feedback. Even though you may not work with friends or family, pose questions to them like these:

- "If I were your boss, what would that be like for you?"
- "What do you think might make it difficult to work with me?"

You can ask similar questions of your coworkers, but your friends and family are more likely to be completely honest with you. I am fortunate enough to work with both my sister and my wife, so I have no shortage of honest, unfiltered, and sometimes blunt feedback coming my way.

You may also have blind spots that are strengths: things you are good at but aren't really aware of. These positive blind spots are also important to consider, as you may be missing opportunities or ignoring areas you might want to explore. To find hidden strengths, ask yourself questions like:

- Where have I been surprised by positive feedback? What are the patterns?
- On what kinds of projects or tasks do people typically ask me for support? What do they have in common?

THE ISSUE OF POWER AND FEEDBACK

You have power, and your staff is aware of this. Power inherently affects the process of soliciting feedback from staff. Unequal power typically distorts feedback. It creates a level of caution – or at worst, fear – in those who are asked to give feedback to a leader. Few people want to risk hurting or offending a person who holds power over them.

Getting honest and direct feedback can be difficult, particularly if there isn't a high level of trust between you and your employees. If a leader doesn't genuinely care, then the process of exploring weaknesses will often end badly for everyone involved. Focusing on weaknesses, and blind spots in particular, requires a leader to be curious, care, and want to know more about what they don't know.

WHO ARE YOU?

Who are you? Really! What makes you tick? What gets you going? What are you good at? What are you bad at? How do others perceive you? *Self-aware leaders continually ask themselves these questions. They are curious, they seek out information and welcome the answers.*

ANOTHER LEADER'S INSIGHTS

CARL HEAMAN-WARNE, Aurora Family Therapy Centre
Carl is the director of therapy at a family therapy clinic. He is part of a leadership team that provides direction to 10 staff. Carl is also a teacher and support person for over 80 graduate students. He is an intuitive leader who highly values the importance of self-awareness in leadership.

We all know that we have strengths and weaknesses, but it takes courage, it takes guts, and it takes honesty with ourselves to explore them. Whether we acknowledge them or not, the people we lead know our strengths and weaknesses in spades. And so, if we are serious about leading, we have to know ourselves inside and out at least as well as our staff do – and hopefully a little bit better.

Being able to acknowledge their challenges actually makes people more competent leaders, and it makes other people have more confidence in them. That type of leader galvanizes respect around them. Leaders who are able to acknowledge their challenges with confidence and continue moving forward – those leaders inspire us.

There are tons of ways to be consistently mindful about who we are and how we come across to others. Be your own detective. Start to just watch how people respond to you. Who are the people coming closer? Who are the ones keeping their distance? What makes people's eyes start to glaze over when you're talking? Where are the little warning bells in the back of your head, and when do they start to go off? Pay particular attention to when people are obviously taking courage to tell you something. Really appreciate the people who tell it to you like it is.

Arrogance becomes a real block for effective self-awareness. If I'm the cat's meow, if I am the be-all and end-all, and I'm the one who's right – organizations with these types of narcissistic leaders become hamstrung. The leaders of these organizations can't see their own challenges and weaknesses, and therefore their personal challenges and their personal weaknesses become the organization's challenges and weaknesses.

I train therapists, and one of the things I teach them is that you can only go as far with clients as you, as a therapist, have gone with yourself. When I look at organizational leaders, I think the same principle applies. An organization will only get so far, and then where the block is in the leader, the organization will also be blocked at the same place.

Self-awareness requires a huge amount of personal intimacy, and there are a lot of us who don't want to be that intimate with ourselves. Leaders who cannot face their own vulnerabilities or weaknesses cannot allow themselves to plan around their weaknesses.

Vulnerability makes a leader approachable. But when leaders are being vulnerable, they need to be careful not to overshoot the mark. The leader who falls apart admitting his or her mistake, and starts to beg and grovel to have the respect of their staff back, may start to undermine themselves as a leader. Leaders need to be vulnerable with a purpose.

It is better to acknowledge where the weakness is, and what impact the weakness has had, and then move on. If you crumble or fall apart, or you abdicate your leadership role and become a peer, your staff may stop seeing you as a leader. Self-awareness doesn't mean that the more you beat yourself up, the more self-aware you are.

Our lives are a process of coming into awareness. I don't think this is a process we are ever done with. The moment we think we're done is often the moment we're hitting a blind spot.

—*Carl Heaman-Warne*

QUESTIONS FOR REFLECTION

This chapter has already posed more self-reflection questions than other chapters. Here is a summary of some of the questions asked throughout the chapter.

1. What are your relational strengths and weaknesses?
2. What are your operational strengths and weaknesses?
3. Who could you ask for feedback about your strengths and weaknesses?
4. What are you doing or could you do to mitigate the negative impact of your weaknesses?

To explore more questions related to self-awareness, review the Leadership Strengths and Weaknesses Assessment in the Resources section, page 191.

5

TALENT AND TEAM SELECTION

● ● ● ● ● ● ● ● ● ●

IT'S ABOUT THE PEOPLE

Organizations are who they hire. Whether an organization succeeds, or even survives, ultimately comes down to the talent and cultural fit of the people who work there. I work hard, I am dedicated, and I am a driven leader, but I can't run my organization alone. Much of what we have accomplished as an organization is a result of who we have hired.

It is clear to me that employee talent drives organizational success, and I am not alone in this belief. When more than 1,000 CEOs were asked which sources of competitive advantage were most important for sustaining their growth over the long term, their number one response was "access to, and retention of, key talent."[1]

The importance of talent acquisition for these CEOs suggests that hiring is not something to be taken lightly or simply outsourced to someone else. Acquiring key talent has momentous consequences, and as a leader it is your responsibility to ensure that hiring is done well.

● ● ● ● ● ● ● ● ● ● ● ● ● ● ● ●

LEADER SURVEY RESPONSES

"People are always the problem, and people are always the answer."

"Hire people smarter than you and listen to them."

"Hire people who excel at the things you don't."

● ● ● ● ● ● ● ● ● ● ● ● ● ● ● ●

THE TALENT SHORTAGE MYTH

It's easy for an organization to blame bad hiring experiences on a shortage of talented people to draw from. In recent years, commentary has increased around the notion that talent is in short supply. I have always had a cynical view of this belief. I don't think there is as much talent shortage as some would have us believe.

I have come to understand that the issue is not so much a talent shortage as it is a shortage of great places to work. Talented employees have choices, and all things considered, they will choose an organization that is great to work for over a lot of other benefits, sometimes including higher pay.

People want to work in organizations that are healthy, innovative, and inspiring. An employee who took part in our survey noted it this way: "With my qualifications and education, I could be making more money, but I stay here because I am valued, I enjoy the work, and I love the people I work with." *Talented individuals seek out great organizations – they won't settle for less, and they don't have to.*

Employers are prone to complain that there is a talent shortage when they can't find someone with the *exact* background they desire and who has the *precise* skills to do the *specific* task they want done. Employers who think this way need only shift their perspectives slightly and focus on aptitude instead.

I have experienced how one of our new employees with a natural aptitude and talent (but not an *exact* match) quickly developed the skill set to do what we needed. I had planned on it taking a year for her to be functioning at the level I desired, but in only a few months, she had the very skills and experience that were needed. Her natural aptitude for the role was so high that she quickly mastered the complexities of the job.

Specialized talent often costs more, and frankly, it deserves more money. Employers may complain of a talent shortage when they can't find someone they desire at the price they would like to pay. If employers are not willing to pay for talent, that does not equate to a talent shortage.

Great talent is sometimes hidden, but the good news is that people with talent tend to know each other. The best talent is often found through referrals, networking, and building relationships. The kind of talent you need is not always looking for work, so job ads are often an insufficient way to find superior employees, and they should not be your only source. When looking to find hidden talent, look for it in nontraditional ways and be sure to tap into your networks.

The reality is that talent surrounds us. If you believe there is a shortage of talent, you are likely missing opportunities.

QUALITY OVER SPEED AND COST

Most leaders I meet are like me when it comes to hiring new employees: We dislike the process, and we would rather be working on far more "important" and "interesting" tasks. Yet the irony is that our organizations won't be successful without the right people in place.

When leaders don't value the hiring process, we risk costly mistakes. While leaders don't need to participate in every hiring decision, they should recognize the importance of talent and lay the framework for how new people are brought into the organization.

Too often, speed and cost are considered the most important indicators of a successful hiring process. Yet the hiring of new employees needs to be much more thoughtful and intentional than simply finding adequate people to fill jobs as quickly or cheaply as possible.

When efficiency is the barometer of success, poor decisions are often made. Instead, we need to center the hiring process on how to reliably find the right people for the right roles – candidates who will not only excel at the job but also fit the organization's culture. *Quality and fit are more important than speed and cost.*

REPEAT

Early on in our organization's life, my wife and I did it all. I was the trainer, the marketer, and the training material developer. My wife, Heidi, provided technical and client services support, answered phone calls, managed our computer systems, and did all the invoicing. It wasn't long until we needed more help.

When we brought new people into our organization, we followed a standard pattern. We would place ads in various publications, weed through the resulting résumés looking for promising applicants, and ask the top three candidates to come in for an interview.

We were often disappointed with who we had to choose from, but we had already spent more time and money on the process than we had planned, so we selected the most promising candidate and hoped for the best. I imagine this process may sound familiar to some of you.

In fairness to our process at the time, we did periodically find exceptional employees. Unfortunately, we also got our fair share of employees who were a poor fit, unethical, or mean-spirited, who had a poor work ethic, or who were simply mediocre talent. In spite of our bad experiences, we continued to use this process for years. When things didn't work out, we would quickly hit the "repeat" button and go through the same poorly designed process again. Thankfully, we have since become more intentional about our hiring process.

FOCUS ON CULTURE

Before organizations can hire effectively, they must be able to clearly articulate what their culture is like. Every organization has its unique culture – a personality, if you will. This culture is made up of elements such as the organization's values, mission, leadership style, and expectations for how employees treat customers, clients, and each other. Organizational culture flows from the values and beliefs that guide how people behave and interact.

While leadership can set the tone for culture, it is ultimately the collection of everyone in an organization that truly defines its culture. Organizational culture is distinct; no two cultures are the same. Howard Schultz of Starbucks makes this point succinctly in his often quoted remark: "We have no patent on anything we do, and anything we do can be copied by anyone else. But you can't copy the heart and soul and the conscience of the company."

Values are the key to a strong organizational culture. Organizations with values that are clearly defined and truly enacted (and not merely aspired to) are in the best position to hire the right people for their culture.

Values provide the framework for how things are done and how people interact. They are most relevant when leaders promote them as nonnegotiable. While it is good for values to be visible, they need to be more than merely a poster on the wall.

For a reference on developing and understanding values, I encourage you to read *The Advantage*, by Patrick Lencioni. Lencioni believes that "core values are not a matter of convenience. They cannot be extracted from an organization any more than a human being's conscience can be extracted from his or her person. As a result, they should be used to guide every aspect of an organization, from hiring and firing to strategy and performance management."[2]

In our organization, we regularly refer to our values in meetings and performance reviews, and of course during the interview process. They truly guide us in many aspects of what we do.

ACHIEVE AND CTRI CORE VALUES

- **EMBODY: We practice what we teach.** We teach others about respectfulness, effective communication, and conflict resolution. We expect our staff to be likable and have the attitudes and abilities to be respectful, to communicate appropriately, and to manage conflict as it comes up.
- **ENGAGED: We care about being here.** We want employees to want and like to be here. We expect our staff to value positive interactions with their coworkers. We want people who are excited by the purpose of their work with our company.
- **EXCEPTIONAL: We have a diverse skill set, and each of us excels at something.** We want our staff to be able to perform at an above average level in at least one key area. We expect that our employees have skills that can easily be plugged into various projects.
- **PRODUCTIVE: We work hard and get things done.** We have a high expectation that work gets done in a fast and efficient manner. We want our employees to have a strong work ethic that is not dependent on managerial oversight.
- **RECEPTIVE: We are open to feedback and change.** We want our staff to respond to feedback in a non-defensive manner. We expect our employees to receive feedback and integrate the content of the feedback promptly.

ASSESS CULTURAL FIT

A candidate's skills, aptitude, and experience are all important considerations when it comes to hiring, but these factors are less significant than how the new hire fits with the organization's culture. We have learned that it is vital for a new employee's personality, behaviors, and attributes to fit our culture.

If there is not a match, regardless of the skill set, the chances of long-term success will be limited. We believe in this so strongly that we have at times selected candidates who have less experience and skill but fit better within our culture. To be clear, the successful candidates did have the aptitude and drive to become more skilled.

While skills can be learned and improved upon, especially for those with the aptitude for the right skill set, it is very difficult, if not impossible, to train someone to fit your culture. Fit is about personality, attitude, and lived values. These three things are very difficult to change or teach.

The good news is that great talent is also looking for the right fit. High-caliber employees are looking for much more than just a job. They are looking to work in organizations that match their personalities and attitudes. In our new hiring process, we ask candidates to respond to the following question in writing when they apply, and verbally during the interview: "What do you do to contribute to a healthy, vibrant work culture?" Candidates have indicated that they were drawn to apply for a position simply because they saw that question in the job posting. They read the question as an indication that we care about organizational health – and they were right.

TALENT AND TASK

In addition to looking for candidates who fit our culture, we are looking for people who feel positive and excited about the specific work they will be doing. We are looking to ensure that talents and tasks align. Talents are our innate patterned ways of thinking and acting. They are those things we are naturally strong at.

In Marcus Buckingham and Donald O. Clifton's *Now, Discover Your Strengths*, the authors state that leaders should focus on talents and strengths:

Start with the right assumptions, and everything else that follows from them – how you select, measure, train, and develop your people – will be right. These are the two assumptions that guide the world's best managers:

1.   Each person's talents are enduring and unique.
2.   Each person's greatest room for growth is in the areas of his or her greatest strength.

These two assumptions are the foundation for everything they do with and for their people. These two assumptions explain why great managers are careful to look for talent in every role.[3]

When hiring for a specific task, it is important to ensure that a candidate's talents are right for the job. Yes, we still care about skills, experience, and education, but we are most concerned with whether the candidate has the natural aptitude and talent for the work, and whether they will be satisfied doing that work. Skills will be learned quickly if the talent is there.

When you are focused on a specific task that you need a candidate to complete, you are less likely to gravitate to the all-around best candidate: the one with a diverse skill set, multiple talents, and a great résumé, who could work in any division of the organization.

Our natural inclination is to want these people on our team. However, I have found that these types of hires tend to become restless and lose interest in the tasks you have hired them to do. It is far better to focus on a candidate with a clear talent for the task than to risk hiring the all-around candidate who will soon become bored.

HIRING FOR BOTH CULTURE AND TASK

When organizations hire people who fit both culture and task, turnover decreases because employees are happy with both their place of work and their task. In contrast, if you are looking for an employee for a customer service department and hire someone whose strengths are marketing or logistics, they are not going to be satisfied with their job, even if they are a cultural fit, because their natural talent lies elsewhere.

If you are a large enough organization, you may consider hiring someone based solely on cultural fit, and then finding a position for them. Jim Collins calls this getting "the right people on the bus." He writes:

> Look, I don't really know where we should take this bus. But I know this much: If we get the right people on the bus, the right people in the right seats, and the wrong people off the bus, then we'll figure out how to take it someplace great.[4]

Most small to medium-sized organizations don't have this luxury, so hiring becomes a process of assessing candidates who fit for both culture and task.

Since the phase in our organization's history when we struggled to find the right talent, our hiring process has become much more focused, and as a result, more successful.

First, as discussed earlier, we are clear about our core values. These may seem far removed from the hiring process, but if you know your core values before you hire, they can be integrated into the interview process and are more likely to be reflected in the person you hire.

We then take time to clearly identify our needs and the skills required for the position. Our goal is to succinctly define the tasks employees will be fulfilling. The end result is a job title, description, and posting that, while short, speaks clearly to both our organizational culture and the tasks of the job. An example of one of our job postings can be found in the Resources section, page 193.

Before formally posting the position, we notify our own networks of the job opening. Some of our employees, in particular our senior employees, have come to us through networking. Our networks and the networks of our current employees are often a rich source of referrals. Remember, talent is sometimes hidden and needs to be found.

INTERVIEWING FOR FIT

In our organization, the first round of interviews is done by an experienced senior employee who has a good understanding of both our culture and the tasks that need to be done. Around 10 applicants are shortlisted using mostly traditional frames of reference:

- Did they use correct grammar and spelling in their résumé, and was it well-formatted?
- Did they do what the job posting asked them to do?
- Did they address their cover letter specifically to our organization, or did they use a standard one they send out to all organizations?
- Does their résumé show they have a history of moving from job to job?
- Did they answer the questions we asked them to respond to? Were their responses crafted with care?

Written responses to our questions are often very telling for both content and level of professionalism. The questions we ask candidates to respond to are located in our sample job posting, found in the Resources section, page 193.

After promising candidates have been identified from résumés, short video interviews are arranged. We use video instead of phone so that we can get a better understanding of the candidate by observing body language, not just listening to them speak. The interviews are usually about 10 minutes, and candidates are asked a few pointed questions:

1. Talk about your abilities, background, and interests in the following areas: (specific to each job).
2. What aspects of workplace culture are most important to you?
3. What excites you about the possibility of being the successful candidate for this position?

The goal is to present a list of three to four high-quality candidates who the in-person interviewing team will have a difficult time choosing between. I become very impatient during an interview when I know right from the start that the person is not a good fit. Having one person "weed through" the candidates by first assessing them with video interviews reduces wasted time during the formal interview phase when there are multiple paid people in the room who are taking time away from their other work.

The formal interview usually involves three interviewers. We ask candidates some standard questions that are meant to assess both cultural fit and task fit. Examples of questions can be found in the Resources section, page 195. While scripted interview questions are the guide, interviewers are free to probe and ask follow-up questions that they feel would be beneficial. After the interview, candidates are given a brief tour of the office and introduced to the other staff.

In the next phase, we bring back our top one or two candidates for a deeper assessment and an orientation to the specific tasks of the job. We want to continue to assess for cultural fit and task fit, but we also want the candidate to assess for fit by actually seeing the job they would be doing. We don't want a new hire to be surprised by the type of work they will be doing, so we spend time introducing them to the job in order to give them a clearer sense of the actual tasks.

Issues normally arise when a successful candidate accepts a job only to find out a week into it that it is nothing like they expected. They either don't find the work meaningful, and struggle to excel, or they quit.

Finally, we make a decision about whether to hire a candidate. Most of the time this process works, and we hire an exceptional employee. However, we are not afraid to start over if we have not found the right person. If we do decide to start over, we assess what might have impeded our ability to find a successful candidate the first time.

KEEP THE FOCUS ON CORE VALUES

Through this entire process, we are focused on how well the potential candidates fit our core values. In the job description, video interview, and in-person interview, our core values are front and center. During the first round of interviews, we ask candidates to specifically review our core values and speak to how their values align with ours.

If we are concerned about a particular core value, we may raise that in the interview as an issue of potential concern and ask them to comment. For instance, if we are concerned about how receptive they are to receiving feedback (one of our core values), we will give them feedback in the interview about something, like an error in their résumé, and see how they respond. *Candidates must fit our core values.*

THE LIKABILITY FACTOR

While we don't have formal break times, I am fine with the mini-breaks that happen naturally first thing in the morning and at various points throughout the day. These periods of interaction around life's happenings build connection and community. They make our office a better place to work.

A few years ago, we had an employee who simply put her head down and worked. She had very minimal interaction with anyone. During an annual review, she indicated how frustrating it was that people would talk about personal matters at work. In her mind, there was too much chitchat. We encouraged her, to no avail, to become more engaged with her coworkers. We eventually realized that her preferences were not a good fit for our culture.

In our hiring of employees, we are also assessing how likeable a person is. Are they enjoyable to be around? Are they someone I could sit next to on a long-distance flight?

We have learned that work environments are much better when we actually like each other and enjoy each other's company. We spend a considerable amount of time at work. Life is so much more enjoyable when workplace interactions are meaningful. While having friends at work isn't always necessary, they sure make the workday more gratifying.

OOPS

Mistakes happen. In spite of our best efforts and processes, it occasionally becomes apparent after a period of time that someone we have hired is not a good fit. They may not fit the culture, or they may not be a good fit for the tasks. Either way, keeping them on and trying to make it work is a disservice to them, their coworkers, and the organization.

As much as we try to help them or make them fit, the reality is, they don't. They may start saying the right things or even try harder. You may coach, encourage, and support them, but in the end, the necessary changes and fit just don't happen.

Historically, in our organization, when we made hiring mistakes, we would focus on the coaching, encouraging, and supporting phase for too long. In spite of our best hopes and efforts, the process of trying to make the person fit rarely worked.

We have learned that if you don't see authentic improvement in the areas of concern quickly, change is not likely to occur. If change doesn't occur, it is better to end the relationship swiftly rather than continue trying to make it work.

When it becomes clear we have made a mistake, we end the relationship as supportively and gently as we can. Instead of quickly moving on to the hiring process again, we carefully assess, analyze, and debrief the situation. What did we miss during the hiring process? What can we learn from this? What will we do differently next time? *Mistakes happen. Fix them quickly, learn from them, and move on.*

HIRING FOR SENIOR POSITIONS

Our approach to hiring for senior positions has been more targeted. When hiring our senior employees, we don't post the job or do a video interview. In one case, the process of courting and hiring happened over a period of close to a year, and in another it occurred over several years.

In both of these situations, I already had a relationship with the individual. One of them had been working with us for several years on a contract basis, and I had known the other as a friend since college. These two people were not looking for jobs when I approached them, and they would not have found a typical job posting.

I believe that leaders should always be on the lookout for talent and nurture relationships with people who may be needed in the months or years ahead. This is especially true when it comes to hiring senior leaders.

Being able to trust those in senior positions is of key importance to me. This is why I find it vital to establish a relationship before hiring for senior positions. Furthermore, I'm looking to hire people who add value in areas I do not. I am looking for people who complement my strengths and cover for my weaknesses.

When it comes to hiring senior staff, you should not be afraid to look for people who are different from you. If you hire senior people who are too similar to yourself, people who share your exact strengths, weaknesses, and perspectives, you are potentially doing your organization a disservice. When you hire people who are different from you in some areas, your organization becomes diversified and better positioned to face both the opportunities and the challenges that lie ahead.

KEEP THE TALENT

Now that you have talent, keep it! Most leaders have, at some point, felt both the direct and indirect impacts of employee turnover. While the direct costs (advertising, interviewing time, training time, etc.) vary depending on a variety of factors (industry, position, location, etc.), it is estimated that the actual costs associated with employee turnover range from 16 to 213 percent of the position's salary. A Center for American Progress study found average costs to replace an employee are

- 16 percent of annual salary for high-turnover, low-paying jobs (earning under $30,000 a year),
- 20 percent of annual salary for mid-range positions (earning $30,000 to $50,000 a year), and
- up to 213 percent of annual salary for highly educated executive positions.[5]

Indirect costs include loss of intellectual capital, disruption in operations, and – in some cases – disturbances to client relations. Especially for small organizations, the loss of a single employee can be very difficult. They may be the only person with a particular skill or knowledge that is very specific and important to the organization.

Keeping talent begins with hiring the right people in the first place. It is also related to most of the other principles reviewed in this book. Motivation and employee engagement, creativity and innovation, and organizational health all impact employee retention.

In particular, I believe that keeping talent relates strongly to organizational health. Most employees want to be in healthy workplaces, and those who have worked in toxic environments are not keen to leave a healthy one, even for a nominal salary increase. While salary may be part of a turnover problem, it is rarely the key thing.

Keeping talent also relates to performance reviews or, as we call them, annual goal-setting meetings. These meetings are the time to assess how people are feeling and fitting in. Have their tasks evolved and changed for a better or worse fit? Perhaps, in their view, the organization's culture has changed for the worse. Maybe they are no longer satisfied in their role and are seeking some variation. Use these intentional conversations to discuss fit as it relates to both task and culture. With an eye on retention, be prepared to make changes based on these findings.

In spite of our best efforts, people move on from time to time, and sometimes for very good reasons – to move to a new city or to go back to school, for example. In our organization, it is the junior staff who are more likely to leave, simply because of where they are in life.

We understand this, and in fact we encourage and even assist our employees in following their dreams, whether that means going to school or traveling the world. However, we have built a culture where we rarely get only the standard two weeks' notice from employees who are leaving. Instead, staff feel safe talking about and planning for their departure with us. The ability to transition over a longer period of time has greatly minimized our indirect costs of employee turnover.

● ● ● ● ● ● ● ● ● ● ● ● ● ● ● ● ●

EMPLOYEE SURVEY RESPONSES

"Leaders in *every* organization in *every* field need to realize that their organization is only as strong as their employees."

"Employees are any organization's largest asset and should be treated like it."

"Good leaders are able to recognize and nurture talent."

● ● ● ● ● ● ● ● ● ● ● ● ● ● ● ● ●

TALENT IS KEY

Attracting, developing, and retaining talent needs to be a key function of leadership, as talent is fundamental to organizational success. Talented people crave workplaces that encourage them to reach their potential, and in that process, they help the organization reach its potential.

....

ANOTHER LEADER'S INSIGHTS

SHAWN MCLAREN, St. John Ambulance
Shawn is the director of operations and learning for a regional office of a national not-for-profit organization. He leads a team of 10 employees, 65 contract instructors, and 300 volunteers. Shawn believes in hiring great people who fit the values and culture of the organization.

Early on in my career, I received the following advice: "Surround yourself with good people." That's something I've tried to adopt in every management position I've had. I believe you need to surround yourself with good people, with passionate people, and then not be afraid to delegate to them.

The very worst thing to do is to just hire a body. I've seen over the years how settling doesn't work. In the hiring process, I'm not afraid to say, "No, let's start again." If you settle, it's usually a complete waste of time, and all you're going to do is cause disruption and conflict with the group you already have.

I hire for passion and personality rather than skill. There's a base amount of skill you want, but in my opinion, there isn't a skill that can't be taught or learned – I really believe that. But it's exceptionally difficult to teach someone to have the type of personality you want them to have.

I've always tried to take the approach that I measure people in two ways: level of willingness and level of skill. If you have both, then fantastic, but if I have one person who has a high amount of skill but a low amount of willingness, and I have someone who has a high amount of willingness and a low amount of skill, I'll always hire the person with more willingness.

Someone who has a high willingness – that's a person who

....

wants to try, who wants to learn. On the opposite side, you get your solo flier who has a high skill level but a low willingness to adapt and learn, to be part of the culture you're trying to create.

When interviewing, I focus a lot on team dynamics. I don't want a whole lot of examples of what they've done in the past because I find those are a lot of prepared answers. So I try to have them talk to me about what their ideal workplace looks like. I'm not so much judging them on their answers as I am judging them on the interaction.

I try to engage applicants in a conversation to find out what they're really passionate about, and then to see if their passions, their personal lives, and their business lives match up with the passions that we're after here. I figure that if they can make the connection between the day-to-day function of their potential job and the bigger picture of what we do, they would make a good employee for this organization.

In hiring for senior positions, what I like to focus on is the "people" aspect. You have to surround yourself with good people, and if a leader gets that, it removes a lot of the fears about your people getting better than you are at certain things. I think that's still out there – we still see some managers who will hold people down, who don't want their coworkers to be better at things than they are, which I think is a massive mistake.

You want to hire senior leaders who have the drive, passion, and commitment to take time to make sure their people are being developed because, in my opinion, that's how you keep people around. If people see that there's room for growth, and that their leadership believes in development, those people are not only going to stay, but are going to excel.

—*Shawn McLaren*

QUESTIONS FOR REFLECTION

1. How would you describe your current hiring process? Does it focus on finding quality employees, or on speed and cost-efficiency?

2. Has your organization clearly defined its core values? If so, what are they? If not, what are the steps you can take to clearly define them?

3. How are your organization's core values used in your current hiring process? If they are not, how could they become incorporated?

6

ORGANIZATIONAL HEALTH

● ● ● ● ● ● ● ● ● ●

WORST SUMMER JOB

"What's the worst summer job you had in your younger years?" I sometimes ask this question when I'm training or consulting with clients, and practically everyone has a story to tell.

During one summer early in my university years, I worked for a company where I was generally disrespected and frequently the target of mean-spirited jokes. To make matters worse, management was not only aware, they were also complicit in these behaviors. The experience significantly shaped my view of both work and leadership. It caused stress, anger, and frustration both during work and when I was not at work. My motivation to do good work disappeared, and the amount of time, money, and productivity this cost the company was seemingly lost on my employer.

I would only work as much as I had to, and when I was working alone, my productivity would decrease even more. In hindsight, this was my way of "getting back" at my employer for not caring about the health of his organization or me as an individual.

When the summer came to an end, I was all too ready to go back to university. From that point forward, I had a clear idea of the type of organizations I wanted to work for, and they would not be like the one I had worked for that summer.

THE HUMAN IMPACT

Years later, and well into my career as a social worker and counselor, I worked with a client who was in the midst of something similar to what I had experienced that summer long ago. In this case, the toxicity of her work environment and the resulting impact on her life were far greater than anything I had experienced. I vividly remember how she explained her daily process of just getting to work and walking in the door, let alone coping with the workday.

The night before work she would already be anxious. She would take a sleeping pill just to fall asleep and still often wouldn't sleep well. In the morning, as she began getting ready for work, her anxiety would increase. As she drove to work she would begin crying, and by the time she had parked her car she would be sobbing. She would wait until the last minute to compose herself and walk into the office to begin her day.

My client described how she would put a shield around herself and slowly go through the motions of work. The tasks of her job took a back seat to the effort of avoiding interactions with her supervisor and certain colleagues. When she returned to her car at the end of the day, she would cry again for five to ten minutes before driving home – only to begin the cycle again.

The impact of her toxic work environment did not stop there. She had initially come to see me because her relationship with her husband was falling apart. However, not surprisingly, her relationship issues could easily be traced back to the personal impact her unhealthy workplace had on her.

This is a heartbreaking story, and it reveals the extent to which an unhealthy organization can impact an individual life. Unfortunately, in my work as a counselor and now as a consultant, I have heard similar stories far too often.

THE COST OF UNHEALTHY ORGANIZATIONS

By now it should be apparent that my use of the term *organizational health* refers to the emotional well-being of people, as opposed to the physical, financial, or strategic health of an organization. Signs of healthy organizations include high degrees of morale, employee satisfaction, and collegiality. Signs of unhealthy organizations include internal politics, dysfunction, and frequent conflict, resulting in both human and financial costs.

Most everyone I know has, at some point, worked in an unhealthy organization, and many still do. Far too often I hear people commiserating about working in such organizations. Even though some try to make light of their working conditions, it is hard to deny the impact an unhealthy workplace can have on someone's life.

Employees of such organizations are likely to become disengaged – motivation and productivity plummet. At worst an unhealthy organization contributes to poor mental health and personal problems that have lasting impacts beyond the organization's walls. *The human impact of unhealthy workplaces is severe – and that is just the human costs.*

The financial costs for an organization are also significant. While identifying the exact cost is difficult, the impact on the bottom line is undeniable. One global survey of over 5,000 respondents found that avoiding conflict resulted in sickness or absence from work in 25 percent of cases. On average, employees spent 2.1 hours every week – about one day a month – dealing with conflict in some way, and 18 percent of respondents said they were aware of people leaving their organization because of conflict.[1]

These findings demonstrate how unhealthy organizations can result in lower productivity and higher employee turnover – things that cost money. Organizational health matters, and if the human impact is not compelling enough to convince you, then at the very least, the financial impact should.

THE THREE BIG CULPRITS

Based on my own experience and consulting I have done with other organizations, the three most frequent culprits causing unhealthy workplaces are disrespect, conflict, and poor leadership.

Culprit #1: Disrespect

Disrespect is any type of behavior that causes offense to others, such as putting them down, abusing them verbally, avoiding or ignoring them, bullying them, and using negative body language. When there are high levels of disrespectful attitudes and behaviors in the workplace, strong organizational health is impossible to obtain.

Culprit #2: Conflict

Conflict is unavoidable. It is inherent within all organizations and all human relationships. Conflict is not the same as disrespect, though people may behave disrespectfully when in conflict. When workers share a high level of trust and strong communication, conflicts are usually navigated and resolved easily. However, if not dealt with properly, conflict can quickly escalate and damage organizational health.

Culprit #3: Poor Leadership

At the heart of most unhealthy organizations is poor leadership. Unfortunately, disrespectful behaviors and poor conflict resolution skills are sometimes modeled by those in management. Some organizations either directly or indirectly encourage behaviors that lead to disrespect and unhealthy conflict. They may do this because they feel that such environments "increase our competitive edge" or that "survival of the fittest ensures that our employees are the best of the best." I believe these attitudes are shortsighted and counterproductive.

Other times leaders are just oblivious and unaware of what is going on under their watch. They are not so much intentional contributors as they are ignorant or indifferent bystanders.

Regardless of leadership's intent, when it comes to creating a culture of organizational health, the process begins with them. Effective leaders will monitor and protect organizational health. When it is suffering, they will take steps to rectify the situation. *Leadership caring about employee well-being is one of the key characteristics of healthy organizations.*

Unhealthy organizations are host to significant problems related to disrespect, conflict, and poor leadership. All organizations will deal with toxic issues from time to time, but for perpetually unhealthy organizations, it is the frequency and severity of the issues that are the problem. In these organizations, disrespect, unhealthy conflict, and poor leadership are rampant and constant.

ON EMPLOYEES' MINDS

In our survey, 52 percent of employee respondents identified a focus on organizational health as one of the top three principles that are *most important* for them to see in their leaders, second only to motivation. And yet these same employees identified organizational health as the principle that their leaders most often *lacked*.

The importance of organizational health is not lost on leaders either. While not rated as highly as motivation or vision, organizational health is tied with passion as the third most important principle according to leaders, with 36 percent identifying it as one of the top three principles that are most important to them.

Organizational health is a priority especially to employees, and therefore it needs to be a priority for leaders as well. It also should not be lost on leaders that organizational health has a direct correlation to motivation and employee engagement, which was explored in Chapter 1.

● ● ● ● ● ● ● ● ● ● ● ● ● ● ● ●

EMPLOYEE SURVEY RESPONSES

"If leadership doesn't care about its employees, the employees don't end up caring about the job."

"The happier we are, the better we work and the more we commit ourselves to the job."

"Leadership is what makes the difference between a good workplace and an unhealthy one."

● ● ● ● ● ● ● ● ● ● ● ● ● ● ● ●

THE CASE FOR ORGANIZATIONAL HEALTH

I know from experience that leaders have many priorities to juggle. Unfortunately, organizational health often takes a back seat to other responsibilities such as finance, strategic thinking, and marketing. Organizational health is usually thought of as something to get to when all that stuff is done. Making matters worse, leaders will sometimes triumphantly roll out one-off wellness activities, new swanky office furniture, or "bring your pet to work" type days. There is nothing wrong with these efforts, but they are not to be confused with real organizational health.

One of the interesting things I have noticed, both in our own organization and in others, is that when internal politics, dysfunction, and conflict are minimal, working on high priority items is easier. When problems or crises arise, healthy organizations rally and manage situations quickly and efficiently.

While it may seem counterintuitive, focusing on organizational health *first* makes the other tasks easier. *Unlike so many other factors, such as government policy, consumer trends, and the economy, organizational health is something we have control over.*

LIKING WHERE WE WORK

At ACHIEVE and CTRI, one of our beliefs is that *people should be able to like where they work.* (For more information, see our mission, beliefs, vision, and core values in the Resources section, page 188.) While there are other factors that impact whether you like where you work, I believe it begins with organizational health.

One of our core values is to practice what we teach. We teach others how to have a respectful workplace, so we should be respectful ourselves. We help individuals who are in conflict with each other resolve their differences, so we had better have a plan for how to resolve our own conflicts. (For more information about conflict resolution and respectful workplace guidelines, see the Resources section, page 185.)

Organizational health is so intimately connected with who we are as a company that it will always be a priority. Fortunately, we are becoming more successful. Here are some recent comments from our staff about what working in a healthy workplace means to them:

- "I previously worked in an unhealthy organization and found that, regardless of the task I was doing, it was miserable being there. Happiness at work is not as much about the work as it is about being respected by your coworkers and supervisors."

- "Coming from an organization that was toxic, working in a healthy organization makes me actually want to come to work. I am happy to pick up extra tasks or work a little longer because I like what and whom I'm working with."

THE ROTTEN APPLE EFFECT

Most readers will be familiar with the rotten apple effect. You look at a basket of apples and see one rotten apple. You are in a rush, so you don't discard the apple right away. Several days later you come back to the basket and find five other rotten apples – and so it continues.

People who contribute negatively to organizational health are like these rotten apples – their negativity grows and spreads. What starts as a simple disagreement can escalate to a full-blown toxic conflict, paralyzing the staff's ability to focus on anything else.

Furthering the impact is that once there is an issue in one area, it spreads to other places. What was once a healthy organization quickly becomes an unhealthy one, and the negative behaviors and attitudes risk becoming the norm.

Our organization has not always been healthy; nor have we always been as diligent about promoting and protecting organizational health as we are now. Regrettably, the insights I have shared, like so many in this book, have been learned the hard way. We have had our fair share of unhealthy periods. Thankfully, we have learned the importance of prioritizing organizational health.

ALWAYS AN AMBASSADOR

I have come to strongly believe in organizational health. I clearly see the correlation between health and productivity. I am an ambassador for the benefits of healthy workplaces, both internally and externally. However, working on creating and maintaining organizational health is not my strength, and I cannot take full credit for the health of our organization.

This may seem confusing. On one hand, I clearly identify organizational health as a guiding principle, yet it is not something I am particularly strong at creating. I know the value of it, I'm just not great at it. However, Eric Stutzman, one of our senior leaders, is exceptional at making organizational health a part of our everyday work experience. It's his thing – it is what he does, and it is the lens through which he views the world.

This example demonstrates how the 10 insights in this book interact with each other and work together. Self-awareness, organizational health, and talent and team selection are all at work here. Through self-awareness, it became apparent that driving organizational health is not my strength. We used smart team selection to identify Eric as the right person to create and maintain our organizational health.

This interaction of principles shows how these insights are not independent. They need each other. It is through the combined impact of these insights that strength and success are realized.

My role is still to participate in and be an ambassador for a healthy workplace. Just because it is not my strength does not mean I value it any less. I am still accountable to my employees and to myself as a leader for ensuring we have strong organizational health. *You do not need to be the driver of all your guiding principles and insights. But you must see their value and be an ambassador for them.*

• • • • • • • • • • • • • • • •

LEADER SURVEY RESPONSES

"Organizational health is the foundation you build on. If you don't have a healthy work environment, it will have a negative impact on all other aspects of the organization."

"When my staff enjoy coming to work and feel safe to bring up concerns, I find they do a much better job."

• • • • • • • • • • • • • • • •

FROM UNHEALTHY TO HEALTHY

Eric started working with us during our most unhealthy time. He and I quickly went to work improving the health of our organization. One of the tools we used to help us was our Organizational Health Assessment, which we still use in our consulting work with other organizations today (see the Resources section, page 189).

This assessment tool is designed to help leaders understand different problem areas and the extent of unhealthy issues. For example, we ask participants to answer how a statement relates to their experience using a scale of 1 to 10: a 10 indicates they strongly agree with the statement; a one indicates they strongly disagree.

Here are a few examples of these statements:

1. People enjoy spending time with their coworkers.
2. Disrespect and conflict are minimal, and if they arise, they are managed quickly.
3. Problems and issues are discussed openly.

When numerous employees have similar negative responses to a statement, the issues that need to be dealt with become clear. Individual responses can also be instructive when combined with interviews.

Through a series of meetings, interventions, and policy changes, we began creating the foundation of a healthy organization. A key part of this was establishing a better hiring process (reviewed in Chapter 5) to make sure the right people are coming into our organization – people who both value and contribute to organizational health and excel in their roles. New employees are oriented to understand that organizational health is essential, not optional.

Organizational health is something our leadership team continually monitors. At annual goal-setting meetings we ask questions about organizational health. Beyond our formal annual meetings, we periodically check in with employees throughout the year. An important question we ask in our meetings is this: "How are you contributing to a positive work environment?"

When issues arise, we manage them quickly so that the "rotten apple" problem does not spread to other areas. When I say "manage," that doesn't mean we micromanage the process. We believe that if we have hired the right people, they should be able to convey feelings and address issues on their own. We provide coaching when someone needs help or is unsure of how to proceed.

A leader's role is not always to intervene directly; more often it is to coach someone about what to do or say. When necessary, a joint meeting to help everyone talk through issues might occur. The goal is to address issues as they come up and before they do too much damage to organizational health.

A BETTER PLACE TO WORK

To achieve maximum success, leaders must value organizational health. Yes, organizations must be innovative and visionary, but they must first be healthy. This takes hard work and requires constant attention, but the payoff is worth it. *Healthy organizations are simply better places to work, and in turn, more good work gets done!*

ANOTHER LEADER'S INSIGHTS

JOHN NEUFELD, House of Friendship

John is the executive director of a multiservice social agency with 150 employees who provide services to over 40,000 people each year. John is passionate about the importance of fostering healthy workplaces.

There is a massive human cost when an organization is unhealthy. Unhealthy organizations have a culture of fear, a lack of innovation, a lack of communication, and a lack of trust that is everywhere.

My big wake-up call that told me I needed to spend more time on organizational health was when someone said to me: "Under your watch, people are being bullied; people are being mistreated." What do you as a leader say to that? None of us value disrespect or conflict that has escalated to unhealthy levels. However, what you don't address, you are basically endorsing. If organizational health is not going well – people are not dealing with conflict, or people are being disrespected – and you as a leader are not doing anything about it, then you are basically saying "We value disrespect."

As a leader, if I knew somebody was crying in the parking lot or being anxious every morning before going to work, it would break me. First, on a personal level, it is just not okay. Second, you are not getting the best of the individual. Both the individual and the organization are suffering. Leaders need to step up and say, "This is not okay. On my watch, this isn't going to happen."

Leadership always sets the tone with organizational health. However, I think very few people know how to do organizational health well. It is a hard thing to do – you have to have a unique set of skills to pull it off. If you don't have the skill set, you had better know it's still important and have some idea about how you are going to work at it.

We recently dealt with a very challenging and unique situation. Right away, people went into solution mode. Everyone pulled together. It was a significant problem, but it didn't immobilize us. We didn't spend time pointing fingers. We quickly found the solution rather than becoming angry or bitter with each other. In a healthy culture, we innovate, take risks, learn constantly, and are able to make mistakes.

One of the ways I know we have strong organizational health is that we are attracting ridiculous talent. We are attracting really bright people who we shouldn't be able to afford. However, they want to be here because of how they are treated and because of the health of our organization.

They see there is a purpose in what they are doing. They are allowed to have autonomy, and they are going to get better and better at what they are doing. They are staying motivated and feel invigorated because their gifts and talents are respected.

For me as a leader, these are very concrete outcomes, and I tie it all back to a focus on organizational health and the realization of its importance.

—*John Neufeld*

QUESTIONS FOR REFLECTION

1. What was your worst summer job experience? What did that experience teach you about organizational health?
2. How healthy is your organization? What are the indicators that tell you it is or isn't healthy?
3. What relationships do you see between organizational health and employee engagement?
4. What specific steps could you take to improve the organizational health of your workplace?

7

PRODUCTIVITY

● ● ● ● ● ● ● ● ● ●

WORK SMARTER, NOT HARDER

When I'm talking to my children about their future goals, or when they ask me about my current success or the future of our organization, I often tell them: "The harder I work, the luckier I get." This saying has always resonated with me. I believe goals are rarely achieved by mere luck – there is always work involved. *Although there may be some fortunate timing of events, work is always a prerequisite to success.*

Success is a by-product of working hard. We control so few things in life, but we do have control over our own discipline, attitude, and work ethic. When we have a positive attitude and the discipline to work hard, we give success the best chance to follow.

Productivity is about hard work, but it's also about how we work. Another saying I often refer to is "Work smarter, not harder." I confess that I recite these two sayings so often that my wife and children roll their eyes and say, "Please, not again," when they hear them. Productivity, for both individuals and organizations, should always come down to *what* and *how* we get things done. It's not just a matter of working hard.

I'M SO BUSY

We are all busy. Hardly a day goes by that I don't hear the phrase, "I'm so busy," from someone. It seems that there is never enough time to do everything we have to get done. As the days, weeks, and years go by, our to-do lists get longer, not shorter. Most of us are overwhelmed by the feeling that we have too much to do and not enough time to do it.

Here's the cold, hard truth: We will never catch up. We will never finish the to-do list. There will always be more we could, should, and would like to do. The requests and responsibilities keep piling up. Yet there is only so much time. We each get 24 hours in a day, 168 hours in a week, 365 days in a year, and only one lifetime. That's it. Our time is limited.

What we do have control over is how we prioritize what we do with the time we have. *The art of productivity is not so much about getting things done as it is about getting the right things done at the right time.* The next time you stare at your to-do list in the morning and feel overwhelmed, stop and recognize that there is always enough time to get *something* done. The ability to focus on the most important task, and then complete it, is the key to productivity.

WHAT'S IMPORTANT

I believe the key to my own productivity is my ability to identify, work on, and complete the tasks that matter most. I determine the items that are most important and push myself, and our employees, to complete those tasks on time. I prioritize my work day and our organization's workflow based on the things that matter most.

Our natural tendency is to avoid bigger tasks that take time and energy. Instead, we focus on little tasks – those that can be easily done and checked off our list for a quick dose of satisfaction. Of course getting things done feels good, but in the larger scheme of things, these little tasks are rarely what drive personal or organizational success. Nor do they often bring a lasting sense of satisfaction.

Productivity that *matters* requires us to finish those big tasks. When we are disciplined to work daily, weekly, and monthly on what is important, those tasks eventually do get done. When we jump into tasks that really matter, and resist the temptation to focus on the easy things, we begin to get somewhere – we are now being productive.

One of my favorite authors, Steven Pressfield, is keenly aware of the importance of choosing what to do. He notes:

> The clock is running in my head; I know I can indulge in daily crap for a little while, but I must cut it off when the bell rings. I'm keenly aware of the Principle of Priority, which states (a) you must know the difference between what is urgent and what is important, and (b) you must do what's important first.[1]

Choosing to do what is important means saying "no" to the things that seem urgent – at least for now. As difficult as it can sometimes be, I have had to learn to say "no" to certain tasks and requests on my time. I am constantly weighing new items against those that are already on my to-do list by asking myself, is this a high-value task or a low-value task? Is this merely an urgent task (answering a ringing phone) or an important one (finishing a key project)?

THE TO-DO LIST

Like most busy people, I live by a to-do list. For years I used a *must-never-lose* black book that went with me everywhere until, *gasp*, I lost it. I now use a cloud-based application for this, and *it* promises to never lose my list.

This may seem elementary, but I find writing tasks down to be essential. Something very important to me, which new employees quickly learn, is that I ask them to take notes when we meet. If I give them direction to do something, I need to see that they have written it down. I actually get anxious and fear they will forget my instructions if they don't write them down. I do not trust memory – things must be written. Eventually, staff learn to bring a pen and paper to every meeting.

I have numerous lists that help me stay organized and focused. There are separate lists for what needs to happen today, this week, this month, this year, and within the next five years.

My most important list is the monthly one. This list is where those big, difficult, complex, and most important tasks go. They can rarely be accomplished in a day or even a week; thus, they go on my monthly list.

I am vigilant about getting these items done *this* month – they do not get pushed back to next month. How long I work on evenings or weekends depends on how the tasks on this list are going. It is simply not an option to carry them over to the next month, so I push on until they are complete, regardless of the extra hours required. Completing these tasks on schedule is paramount.

My weekly and daily lists are more fluid. I try to set realistic goals, and I work hard at getting these lists done too, but not at the expense of progress on my monthly goals. If items from these lists don't get finished on time, they move forward to the next day or week, and I don't lose too much sleep over them.

It is important to organize these two lists frequently. Normally, I do so at the end of the day or later in the evening. This allows me to start the next morning with a planned course of action. The list really doesn't take too much time to create, and I truly believe that taking this little bit of time to plan actually makes me more efficient. This list-making keeps me focused and holds me accountable to my goals.

The most productive people I know keep two things at the forefront: goals and action. They know what they want to do, and then they do it.

●●●●●●●●●●●●●●●●

LEADER SURVEY RESPONSES

"You can't be afraid to jump in and do something. Never ask someone to do something that you would not do yourself."

"Walk the walk; be the model for higher productivity."

"Having clear expectations is crucial to success. I don't only mean telling them the expectations, I mean modeling the expectations."

●●●●●●●●●●●●●●●●

I'M NOT AVAILABLE

Breakfast meetings are not for me. If you ask me out for breakfast, I will almost always say no. A morning meeting? Never. I am always booked with "other things". These other things are actually not meetings or events, they are my own tasks. Mornings are my most valuable time, and I use them almost solely for working on my big monthly tasks. My head is down, and I'm focused on my most important priorities.

This book was written in the mornings. When I have to think hard on a task that requires all my concentration and energy, I do it in the morning. The afternoon is my time for having meetings, returning phone calls and emails, and doing smaller, less focused tasks.

This is my natural flow of energy, and I have found the way to harness it. My most important tasks get my attention when I am at my peak. The less pressing tasks, and those that require minimal mental energy, fill in the gaps.

Most of the important work we do requires large chunks of uninterrupted time to complete. Leaders must carve out time specifically for these tasks. Your door should be shut (sometimes literally), and you should communicate that you are not available for meetings or interruptions as you are hard at work on your important items. This is your time, and you must protect it from being hijacked by other people or distractions.

Each of us is different. The best time for me and many others to focus is in the morning. For some people, it may be the afternoon or evening. Find your optimal time and dedicate that time as sacred, for it is in these times that your big tasks will see progress and completion.

PROCRASTINATION AND RESISTANCE

Inevitably, there will come a time when the forces of procrastination and resistance will overcome us. Starting will be harder than it used to be, the final destination will seem further than it was before, and desire and focus will wane.

My key strategy for working against resistance is to have a schedule and stick to it. When I am writing, I start at 8 a.m. every day. I'm not always sure what I'm going to write, but I sit down and start. The process of doing the work at a set time is important, especially when you don't feel like it. When you sit down day after day at your set time to work, ideas will eventually come.

I can only sustain three to four hours of this intense focus before my attention begins to fade. But I know this about myself, and I don't fight it. I just make sure to begin again the next day at 8 a.m. sharp.

Waiting for the right time to start is almost always a sign of procrastination. The perfect time to start a task rarely shows itself. The reality is that we will always be juggling different tasks and demands; there will never be a time when everything is caught up. *We must learn to start and complete tasks in the midst of distractions and chaos.*

People can develop habits and rituals to help them work through their distraction. One of the telltale signs that I am focused and ready to work is my posture. I normally sit in a slouched position, but when I am focused and working, I have perfect posture. I wasn't even aware of it until several observers pointed this out to me.

Although this may sound counterintuitive, I have found that perfectionism can be an excuse for procrastination. An overzealous focus on perfection limits our ability to finish a task because things are never quite right. Perfection is a myth. Things will never be just right; there is always more tinkering one could do. *Perfectionism is just something that keeps people from finishing their work.*

BE REALISTIC

Some tasks take months or even years to complete. They require methodical planning and realistic time frames. I often encounter people who have realistic goals but overambitious time frames for completing their tasks. When things do not work out as planned, these people are more prone to give up or fail.

Some tasks are so ambitious, and their scope so grand, that adequate schedules must be allocated for them. The writing of this book, and its development into the form you see now, took 18 months from start to completion. This book did not come to be through some ill-conceived notion that it would be easy or quick. Instead, it took methodical planning and step-by-step completion of smaller tasks to turn it into reality.

When you set about to complete a major task, begin with the end in mind and consider all the steps that will be required along the way. Focus on pacing yourself, for you will need stamina to make it to the end. Set about a process of methodically and intentionally working toward your end goal.

If you push too hard for too long, you are at risk of crashing. Picking back up again after taking a long break will be far more difficult than if you had set realistic goals from the start. Furthermore, if you stop working toward a goal for too long, you may never actually start again.

PINGS, PONGS, AND MULTITASKING

Uninterrupted time is key. Picking up where you left off after even a minor interruption takes more time than most of us realize. The process of starting and stopping, leaving and coming back, putting down and picking up, takes a big toll on our efficiency.

Productivity is not enhanced by multitasking. The effectiveness of multitasking is largely a myth. We are capable of doing more than one thing when it comes to automatic activities like walking, washing dishes, or sweeping the floor. However, when it comes to tasks that require high levels of conscious thinking, there is no such thing as multitasking – only task switching.

When we think we are multitasking, we are really doing no more than switching back and forth between multiple tasks with far less efficiency – and likely far less accuracy – than if we had focused on one thing for a longer period of time.

Less obvious forms of multitasking are the "pings" and "pongs" of our various devices that interrupt our flow – those various annoying noises our phones and computers make to announce the arrival of a new email or tweet. Even if we don't respond to them right away, there is a momentary switching of tasks that takes place in our brain.

EMAIL TIME-SUCK

A study by McKinsey Global Institute found that the average worker spends 28 percent of their time at work either reading, writing, or responding to emails.[2] When I talk to leaders about what takes time away from their tasks, email is always near the top of the list. I also believe email takes up more of my time than it should.

It's important to note that everyone's approach to taming email will be different. I'm not organized or tech-savvy enough to have color codes, multiple files, or self-sorting rules. I have, however, developed the following habits and rules that help me keep my email under control:

- I try to work through my emails daily. I've learned that it's better to respond today than tomorrow, and sometimes better to delete today than tomorrow. For me, keeping a clean inbox with minimal emails waiting for my response is key.

- I ask to stop being cc'd if I view the email thread as not relevant to me. This reminds people to consider whether or not they should include me the next time they start an email thread.
- When I receive an email that should have been directed to someone else, I take time to explain to the person why they should have sent the email to someone else. This short amount of coaching results in fewer unnecessary messages directed to me in the future.
- I write short emails. Longer emails usually take more time than brief phone conversations. If an email will take more than five minutes to compose, I'll use the phone instead.
- I do not hold "meetings" over email, and if I am drawn into one, I am quick to shut it down. When an email turns into a back-and-forth conversation, I ask for a phone or in-person meeting instead.
- A new strategy I am currently in the midst of is unsubscribing from the countless newsletters I receive. In the past, I have just deleted these emails daily instead of taking the time to unsubscribe from them.

Email is a great tool. It can, however, feel like an all-encompassing battle to manage. Be mindful that without good habits and a system for dealing with it, email will quickly get in the way of your productivity.

THE DREADED MEETING

In addition to emails, meetings are frequently mentioned in my conversations with leaders as a source of frustration and a barrier to productivity. Meetings do take time, and sometimes it feels like that time is wasted. However, meetings are essential for sharing information, making decisions, and fostering innovation.

We can't get rid of meetings; they are here to stay. But we can reduce the time we spend in meetings through better planning. Two key questions I keep at the forefront are:

1. Why are we having the meeting?
2. Who should be at the meeting?

People often hold meetings for the sake of meeting. There is a Monday morning meeting because, "well, there has always been a Monday morning meeting – that's when we meet". In reality, the meeting may not be needed.

First, we must be clear about the purpose of our meeting and consider whether we even need to meet at all. Second, it is important to be clear about who should be at the meeting. If only a few people speak at a meeting, this is a sure sign that there are too many people there.

Unless the meeting is happening for purely informational purposes, all employees present should have something to contribute. I have found that it is usually best to have frequent, smaller, and shorter meetings with the right people as opposed to larger, longer meetings with the wrong people.

When meetings are planned thoughtfully and facilitated effectively, they can be extremely helpful for enhancing the productivity of an organization. Meetings should be a tool for productivity, not a hindrance.

THE HOURS WE WORK

A quarter of the population say they work 45 to 50 hours each week, and about a third indicate that they work more than 50 hours a week.[3] At the higher end of the spectrum, a study by Gallup found that 12 percent claim to work more than 60 hours each week.[4]

I believe productivity is more tied to *how* we work than the number of hours we work. However, as long as we can stay focused and work at a high capacity, we can conceivably be more productive working 50 hours a week than 40. It is also possible for someone working

30 hours a week to be more productive than someone who works 50, simply because of *how* they work.

Most of us can also work beyond our normal capacity for a few weeks if needed. For me, this typically occurs when I'm pushing hard to finish a project – having the end in sight gives me the stamina to power through. I am able to stay focused because I am excited to finish, and I also realize the extra effort is only temporary.

I believe we must be mindful in considering why we work as much as we do. Your own situation is unique, and the hours you work may be a good fit for you. However, in my experience, I have seen a lot of people who are busy for the sake of being busy.

Many of us experience a natural sense of satisfaction when we are busy. We feel needed and important. Yet busyness can be a distraction that prevents us from working on the things that matter most. *Productive people see busyness not as a sign of importance, but as a possible sign of laziness, lack of focus, or wasted energy.*

If people are too busy, what are they doing wrong? Why aren't they figuring out how not to be busy? Being busy keeps us from concentrating fully on the few tasks that are essential for us to do. In the often quoted words of Henry David Thoreau, "It is not enough to be busy; so are the ants. The question is: 'What are we busy about?'"

THE *IDEAL* AMOUNT OF WORK?

It's difficult to quantify the exact relationship between the number of hours we work and the cutoff when our productivity begins to slip. Most of us can identify that there is a certain point when our productivity falls off sharply. My limit tends to be working nine hours in a day. Some recent research found that our work output falls sharply after a 50-hour work week, and falls even more drastically after 55 hours.[5]

There are exceptions, but for most people, productivity begins to decline after eight or nine hours of consecutive work. If we push beyond a certain point, we end up accomplishing less in the last hour of work than we did in the first hour.

Currently, I am content with my work schedule. My normal work week is 55 hours in total. On several evenings throughout the week, I work for one hour responding to emails and organizing my next day. I usually work one morning on the weekend. This allows me to get an extra block of high-productivity time into my week. I take five weeks of vacation a year, during which I respond to emails for 30-60 minutes a day. I also work reduced hours, away from the office, for another five weeks.

What's most important is that this daily and weekly rhythm works for me. I'm content, my family is content, and I have enough time to follow my other passions. There have been times when I have pushed closer to 60 hours a week, and that's too much for me. Those extra hours slowly take their toll. I'm not able to get to my other passions, my wife begins to resent my long hours, and the joy of my work wanes.

The leaders I interviewed for this book all have their own unique work schedules. John Neufeld, whose insights are shared in Chapter 6, works 50 hours a week and takes four weeks of vacation a year in which he is completely disconnected from the office. On evenings and weekends, he only does event-based work like attending board meetings and fundraising events. Jeff Schmidt, whose insights are presented in Chapter 1, works more than 60 hours a week, but he gets a whopping 13 weeks of vacation! He regularly works evenings and weekends when he's not on vacation.

What's interesting to note is that John, Jeff, and I all structure our work schedules differently, but the annual average of hours we work is actually very similar. While most leaders I interviewed work at least 50 hours a week, there is no standard to adhere to other than the one you create for yourself.

FARMERS' HOURS

There is a saying in the farming community: "Farmers do more by 9 a.m. than most people do all day." I told you about my brother's passion for farming in Chapter 2. But not only is he passionate, he also works longer and harder than most people I know. He's up early almost every morning to milk cows, and he works late into the evening planting, haying, and harvesting nine months out of the year.

From April to October, he works 80 hours a week, and during the other five months, he works 60 hours a week. He takes one week and several weekends off each year. His capacity and willingness to work long hours are beyond my own or that of most leaders I know. The hours my brother works are extreme and rare. What's most interesting, though, is that he keeps these hours year after year. They don't break him down; he's actually happier than most people I meet who work 40 hours a week. He loves his work and does not begrudge the hours.

While I caution against working extreme hours, the reality is that some people are able to do so with minimal side effects. I think this is the exception more than the norm. The farmers I know often refer to their vocation as their "way of life." Their passion for their land and animals, combined with the personal satisfaction gained from this life, means that they don't think about work in terms of hours.

Peter Loewen, whose insights are shared in Chapter 8, also works "farmers' hours." For the months of April to October, he works 85 hours a week, and for the other five months, 40 hours. He takes three to four weeks of vacation a year, but on vacation and weekends, he is always available.

Similar to my brother, Peter is content with this work and life. When I asked him about the magnitude of his work hours, he responded with a simple explanation: "It's a good life."

SLEEP AND HEALTH

When people work too many hours, their health usually suffers. They are more prone to eat poorly, sleep less, and forgo exercise. A key characteristic that I have found in many high-performance leaders is that they are healthy. They exercise, eat well, and get the sleep they need. People who are healthy simply feel better, have more energy, and get more work done.

My wife is adamant that our kids eat a good breakfast – especially on days when there are sporting events or tests. She makes sure the kids have a breakfast that includes protein and healthy fats because research shows these will keep you feeling fuller for a longer time and give you the energy your brain needs to function at peak performance.

Interestingly, a person can go a week without eating, and while they will be uncomfortable and lose weight, they will still be able to function. Sleep, on the other hand – give that up for a few days and you will be disoriented and unable to function. Despite this, there is a notion that high performers are those who trade sleep for work — that sustained exhaustion is a rite of passage for leaders. I don't believe this to be true at all!

Sleep is vitally important. I need more than most in order to function well, especially since I sustained a concussion while mountain biking. I regularly get at least eight hours, and I often get nine hours a night. This helps me to start my day fresher and think more clearly. I'm more productive and a better leader because of it.

LEADING FOR PRODUCTIVITY

When I walk into other high-performing organizations, the atmosphere is palpable. You can feel it. Instead of just going through the motions, people are working intentionally and purposefully. Employees are confident in their leaders and themselves. Work is getting done quickly, efficiently, and well.

The challenge for a leader is not just to sustain one's own productivity but also to help employees, and by extension the entire organization, become more productive. One way of helping employees is by modeling productivity. If you want to create a culture of productivity, show up and work. Be an example for others to emulate.

At ACHIEVE and CTRI, productivity – working hard and getting things done – is one of our core values. We demand that our employees and organization be productive. We do not accept mediocrity. When you have staff who can't pull their weight, you risk bringing other employees, and the organization, down.

Leading a culture of productivity is intimately connected to the concepts that were reviewed in Chapter 1, on Motivation and Employee Engagement. These two insights are very intertwined. You can't have a highly productive workforce without motivated and engaged employees.

First, focus on motivation and employee engagement – productivity will follow. Productivity is the result of engagement and good habits. We can share insights with employees, and we can teach them habits and techniques to make them more productive, but this is not helpful unless employees are engaged and motivated to work hard in the first place.

● ● ● ● ● ● ● ● ● ● ● ● ● ● ● ● ●

EMPLOYEE SURVEY RESPONSES

"If you cultivate loyalty, then work ethic, work quality, and job ownership will follow."

"The biggest key for a workplace to be productive is to have a safe and welcoming environment in which to work."

"When employees are well cared for, they can be more productive."

● ● ● ● ● ● ● ● ● ● ● ● ● ● ● ●

DRIVING PRODUCTIVITY

In my intense focus on my monthly tasks, and in the strictness with which I carve out time for myself to work on projects, there is always a sense of resolve and importance. Tasks must be completed correctly and on time.

I strive to inspire our employees to work with the same level of intensity that I do. I am driven to make our organization better. One of my roles as a leader is to clearly communicate the goals and tasks that are priorities, and then I must encourage employees to achieve them.

When I talk about projects and goals with our staff, I often use the terms *drive, push, fast,* and *hard* to describe how to get work done. We need someone to *drive* this project, we all have to *push hard* to see this goal become a reality. We need to *drive fast* to finish this task on time. This drive to push hard and fast is fueled by my sense of resolve. Things must get done *right, fast,* and *on time.*

ANOTHER LEADER'S INSIGHTS

JOE GRIESER, Grieser Dairy Farm

Joe owns and operates a small, organic dairy farm with his spouse, adult children, and several part-time employees. The combination of his passion for farming and his focus on productivity has helped him become a leader to whom new and aspiring farmers look for guidance.

I get smarter about how I work the older I get. In many ways, I feel like I get more done now than I did in my 20s. It's the simple things really. If I'm walking from one place to another, I'll put a pair of buckets down where I can easily pick them up again later in the day without taking extra steps. Simple things like that make a difference in the course of a long workday.

Getting all the work done on the farm requires me to get going early every morning. Pressing snooze on the alarm is not an option. Even when I don't feel like it, I have to get up. If I start chores late, the day's work will never get done. Starting early and getting morning chores done means I can get to my major priorities.

My major priorities each have a date attached to them. The dates are not written down anywhere, but they are all in my head. Oats need to be planted by May 1, barley by May 10, corn by May 25, and so on. Meeting these dates is essential to keep things running smoothly.

Whether I work later at night or longer on the weekends is determined by how far along I am toward reaching these goals. Having a specific date in mind keeps me on target. I think I learned this from my great-uncle – he was always done planting a crop while other farmers were just starting to talk about it. Even in his old age, he would get more work done in a short period of time than most people I know because of his intense focus on getting things done on time, if not early.

In farming, to keep working, you've got to be an optimist because a lot of the time things aren't looking good. Life on the farm is unpredictable, and just when things are going well, machinery breaks down, it doesn't rain, it rains too much, or money is tight.

When things aren't going well, I work to remain positive. I always tell my sons, "It will all work out." With perseverance and continued work, things usually fall into place. But in hard times you do have to keep working. You can't sit still and expect things to work out by themselves.

If you are passionate about farming, even when the times are tough, you are going to make it. Passion and hard work are essential to this lifestyle. Without them you will fail.

—Joe Grieser

QUESTIONS FOR REFLECTION

1. How do you prioritize high-value over low-value tasks?
2. What strategies do you use (or could you use) to create more time to work on these high-value tasks?
3. Is your day or week full of cluttered multitasking, emails, and meetings? What are things you can do to make these tasks less time consuming?
4. Are you happy with the level of productivity in your organization? If not, how can you lead productivity better?

8

CREATIVITY AND INNOVATION

● ● ● ● ● ● ● ● ● ●

MOONSHINING

As children, my siblings and I were very inventive with our play – we were always innovating and creating something or another. Inside the house, LEGO was our main source of entertainment. These weren't the new LEGO pieces with fancy parts and detailed directions. Our LEGOs were basic building blocks that required a vision for what they might become. We would build entire cities and farms with our ever-growing supply of blocks.

We had even more fun outside. Away from the watchful eyes of our mother, our ideas really came to life. We had access to a large supply of tools, a junk pile, and most importantly, a forest in which to explore. Add fire, and things got even more exciting! The combination of these elements created an endless list of things we could do.

One of our most memorable innovations was the construction of a whiskey still for making moonshine. We started at the junk pile to find what we needed for our small still, which was really just a simple metal structure in which to boil water.

We then picked some corn from my uncle's field. Next, we made a big fire to provide the high temperature needed for boiling corn and water in a pot. Finally, we found some mason jars for our finished product, and we began the much anticipated fermentation process.

We waited for the magic to happen, but alas, every time we tried our product, we simply tasted corn soaked in water – which, if you've never tried it, is not particularly refined. Sadly, and despite our best efforts and lots of good fun, the moonshine never came to be.

EMBRACING YOUR INNER CHILD

My siblings and I never had a shortage of ideas, and many of our plans were actually implemented in one form or another. If an idea didn't pan out, we would move on to the next one.

Being curious and creative was natural for us, and if we had an idea, we would pursue it. We didn't second-guess ourselves, delay our plans, or hold meetings to determine budgets. We simply tried things because we were curious and had the desire to create something unique.

My hunch is that you have similar stories of childhood dreams, explorations, and creations. But what about now? Are you still making new stories? As an adult, do you still dream, create, and innovate with the same curiosity you had when you were a child? Regrettably, I have found that many adults have suppressed the curiosity they had as a child.

Great innovators still embrace the curiosity of their inner child. Their lives are not driven by fear. They still have the curiosity, courage, and drive to keep exploring and pushing boundaries. They are still making moonshine, even though they might fail.

WHAT'S NEXT?

What's next? I love those two words. They excite me like few others.

123

What's next! These words speak of possibilities, change, and new frontiers. *What's next* keeps me up at night and gets me up in the morning.

I am an ideas person. I am always thinking, dreaming, and scheming about the future. I am always listening and watching for anything that will spark an idea. I follow my curiosities down winding, hidden pathways – sometimes literally! I ask questions with the inquisitiveness of a child, and I am open to any inspiration that might come my way.

I have learned that if I am not looking for and open to inspiration, ideas simply won't come. Inspiration is not something that just happens on its own. Inspiration needs a willing partner, someone who is listening, who is open to hearing, and most importantly, someone who is willing to give it a helping hand.

When a great idea comes – whether I'm driving down the road, in the shower, or fast asleep – a mystical sensation overtakes me. I'm full of life, energy, and excitement. I am overcome with inspiration, and I can't wait to get started!

FILTER IDEAS

Multiple ideas can come out of the question "What's next?" In reality, we won't be able to pursue them all, nor should we. Some of them will be bad ideas, or they will not be a good fit for our organization.

Ideas need to be filtered, and we need to decide whether to follow them or leave them on the sidelines. Perhaps they will be picked up again at a later point. However, if we set them aside, it is possible that they will be picked up by someone else and we will miss an opportunity.

I use several filters when I'm deciding which ideas to pursue. First, I think about the idea and jot down some notes to help me ascertain whether to follow it or not. I ask myself the following questions:

- Is the idea realistic?
- Would the end result be worthwhile?
- Will the idea distract us from more important projects?

- How will this idea provide value?
- Is there a way to test the idea before fully committing?

If I'm still drawn to the idea, I will then discuss it with other people in our organization. This serves to test my thinking about the value of the idea. After these conversations, the idea will either begin to fade or it will have grabbed hold of me even more. If I'm now firmly committed to it, the real action begins – now I have work to do.

START WORKING

Once ideas have been filtered and I have decided to pursue one, it needs to be enacted. What good is an idea if it remains only a concept, only a possibility? Ideas are meant to be explored and built upon, but they need work.

Start working. Take a step toward bringing your idea to life. Too many people sit on an idea, waiting for just the right time, waiting for a little more clarity before they start. This waiting is often when the inspiration begins to fade.

Ideas that sit there, that are left alone, will soon go dormant and will eventually wither and die. Years down the road, someone else will have implemented the idea – your idea. You will say to your friends, "I had that idea years ago, but I never got around to making it happen." Don't let this be your experience. Now is the time to get to work. Start working when the inspiration is at its highest.

KEEP WORKING

When bringing ideas to life, one does not typically move from one inspirational high to the next. I have found that there is usually an in-between time where unglamorous work needs to happen. Most of my time is spent laboring to make my ideas come to life. I am typing, writing, thinking, preparing, and working on my ideas. I am focused, intentional, and methodical in my work.

I've learned to expect a stage when things are not happening as I had planned and frustration sets in. When these moments come, it is essential to just keep working. Starting the work is the first step; continuing to work through frustration and discouragement is the second. One must work not only when things are going well. *Perseverance in times of frustration is essential to making ideas come to life.*

One of my favorite quotes on the importance of perseverance is attributed to the writer William Faulkner. When asked if he wrote on a schedule or only when struck by inspiration, he is said to have responded, "I write only when inspiration strikes. Fortunately, it strikes every morning at nine o'clock sharp." The meaning being, we must keep working regardless of how we are feeling on any given day.

Unfortunately, many ideas are never manifested because there are a great number of people who never finish things. They begin with the best intentions, but then along the way they slow down and give up – they don't finish what they have started.

So please commit to finishing what you start – enact the idea! You have control over this part. You can keep working. You can choose to work your tail off to bring your idea to life. You can't choose how people will respond to what you complete, but you can choose to finish.

MOVE ON

You have finished! Congratulations! Now the bad news: Regrettably, not all the ideas we bring to life will turn out well. We will have toiled for hours, months, or perhaps even years on end only to find that the finished product didn't turn into what we had hoped or dreamed. Like the failed moonshine of my childhood, our ideas don't always succeed.

One of the most important aspects of establishing an innovative organizational culture is embracing failure as a part of innovation. All innovation involves the possibility of failure. Trying something and failing should be viewed as a learning experience and a part of the process.

So stop sulking! Learn from it and move on to your next idea.

Don't get stuck in your disappointment. Finish what you started, but if it doesn't work, continue on to something else. Don't dwell on your failures, learn from them. *Then move on – always move on to what is next.*

CREATIVITY AND INNOVATION

Our organization follows a planned approach to creativity and innovation, using the process I just articulated. We ask *what's next*, we *filter ideas*, we *start working*, we *keep working*, and then we *move on* if they don't work out. We begin by being open and searching for ideas – the creativity part. Once we settle on an idea, we work to implement it – the innovation part. If an idea fails, we move on.

The terms *creativity* and *innovation* are often used interchangeably, but while you can't have innovation without creativity, you can have creativity without innovation. People often call ideas innovative before the work required to implement them has been done.

Your organization can display creativity when you have a team meeting and develop a dozen new ideas. However, there is no innovation until you do something about those ideas by putting them into action.

Creativity is the process of coming up with new ideas, and innovation is the implementation of those ideas. Creativity is the beginning of a process that has the potential to result in innovation. Innovation takes new ideas and develops them into something useful. Innovation is what brings creativity to life.

Creativity is very important, but it is only the beginning. Yes, organizational success and growth depend on creativity, but it is innovation that brings about the results. *Innovation puts creativity to work and makes it useful.*

TYPES OF INNOVATION

An innovation may be a new product, service, or process. It may be a new way of marketing, improving customer service, or structuring your organization. Every area of an organization has the potential to be improved through innovation, and should be.

A common mistake that organizations make is restricting their ideas and innovations to only new or improved products. Yet every aspect of your organization should be fair game for innovation. Nothing should be sacred.

Innovations can range from incremental changes to major shifts. When you make a minor improvement to any existing product, process, or service, incremental innovation has occurred. Most successful people and organizations are good at incremental innovation, and we often innovate without even naming it as such.

Major innovations, on the other hand, involve doing something entirely new. Major innovations are typically riskier and more difficult to implement. As such, most people and organizations are not as successful or comfortable with implementing major innovations.

INCREMENTAL INNOVATION EXAMPLE

Using technology to improve systems is the most common method of innovation in today's organizations. Our organization provides public workshops. Most of our participants register as individuals or as small groups from various organizations. We process thousands of registrations each year, yet the way in which we process registrations has evolved significantly over time.

Our first website was static – it showed information but did not function as an e-commerce site. We provided information online, but all registration was done by phone or fax. I still remember the excited feeling we would get every time the fax machine rang. It was the sound of another workshop registration. On busy days, our fax line would be tied up, and clients would have to try multiple times to send in their registrations. Looking back, only 10 years later, this process seems painfully inefficient and archaic.

We now have a robust and complex e-commerce website that handles the majority of our registrations. Interestingly, the number of registrations we process has grown astronomically, but the size of our client services team has remained approximately the same.

Over a period of years, through incremental innovation, we have become much more efficient. This is one example of how innovation sometimes happens over a period of years and how the process never really ends.

MAJOR INNOVATION EXAMPLE

Two years after starting CTRI, we made the decision to start ACHIEVE as a second division. It had become apparent that our vision for offering leadership and workplace performance workshops didn't fit together well with the mental health, counseling, and violence-prevention topics for which we were known. We felt we would be better served in the long term by having two distinctly branded divisions.

The idea for ACHIEVE came while I was on vacation with my wife in Key West, Florida, over the winter holidays. Vacations, it turns out, are one of my main idea-generating times.

Over the next spring and summer, we set about creating an entirely new division – building a website, developing training and marketing materials, and hiring staff. We had a few bumps along the way, but we kept working at it. By the fall, eight months after the idea, ACHIEVE was open for business, and it has been thriving ever since.

THE INNOVATIVE CULTURE

Every day, employees have the choice to diverge from the norm and innovate. Employees continually have opportunities to try new things, test processes, and improve efficiencies. These opportunities exist, but are you as a leader making space for them to be explored? Are you building a culture that promotes creativity and innovation?

Innovation should not be the result of a once-a-year brainstorming event. Innovation can and should be a continual process, something that happens every day. My job as a leader is to foster a culture of innovation, to help people think differently – to help people think, period. My goal is not to have our team come up with only one great idea each year, but to create a sustainable and rooted innovative culture – one that is constantly changing and progressing.

In workplace cultures that foster creativity and innovation, employees ask questions and make mistakes without fear of reprisal. Everyone is expected to challenge the way things are done, and everyone is continually focused on how they might do things better. Innovative leaders model this behavior and, in doing so, inspire employees to innovate as well.

●●●●●●●●●●●●●●●●●

EMPLOYEE SURVEY RESPONSES

"I appreciate a leader whose ego allows us to look collectively at the question, 'What can we do better?'"

"I wish my manager would stay current and not insist we do something that *so-and-so* did here 10 years ago."

"I like leaders who are courageous and unafraid to take risks."

●●●●●●●●●●●●●●●●●

WHAT PROBLEMS ARE PEOPLE HAVING?

In our organization, innovation often begins as a response to a problem that a client or a prospective client is having. We listen closely and ask a lot of questions. We request feedback on their experiences with us and ask them to share any problems they may have encountered.

We listen for themes of frustration or concern regarding our products, services, and procedures. For example, we may ask, "What are the pain points for our clients in the registration process or the in-person experience on a day of training?" Out of these conversations and observations, the creative and innovative processes emerge.

A few years after we started offering workshops, we identified that a key problem for remote communities was accessing training in a cost-effective way. At the time, the only way to receive training from us was through in-person workshops.

As a result of identifying that remote communities couldn't access our training in a cost-effective way, we developed a video training platform and webinars, and made our resource manuals available for purchase. We believe training should be accessible to everyone, and we are committed to making this a reality.

WHAT DO PEOPLE WANT?

At the end of the day, the product or service you are providing must be wanted or needed by someone. That is the only way for an organization to survive. Most of our products and services come about as a result of listening to our clients' feedback and providing what they are asking for.

We create entirely new workshops based on the topics our clients request. At its inception, our organization offered only two workshops. Ten years later, we provide training and resources on more than 75 different topics. Each year, we assess changes in the market and gaps in our offerings, then develop new materials to fit those needs.

WHAT DO PEOPLE NEED?

Some of our products and workshop topics are created not because clients ask for them, but because we believe that if we create them, people will realize that they need them. These innovations sometimes respond to a gap or opportunity we foresee due to certain trends, or sometimes they are based on a simple hunch that a product or service could meet a yet to be identified need.

For example, we offer various assessment tools that provide leaders with a guide for having thoughtful and proactive conversations with their employees. We didn't have clients asking for them, but we did have a sense that, if we developed these tools, our clients would find value in them.

Our workshop topics, products, and services result from listening closely and paying attention to the world around us. I read every day – newspapers, magazines, blogs; I read with an eye for upcoming trends. I walk through life constantly curious about how things work. I look for unique stories of businesses and organizations that are doing things I have never thought of before. I encourage this and teach the value of it to our employees as well.

WHAT'S BUGGING YOU?

What's bugging you? What's bugging us? These questions are born out of the "Lean" movement. There are countless books and articles about lean processes, and my intention here is not to provide an exhaustive analysis. What I value about the contribution of lean principles to innovation is the emphasis on becoming less wasteful and more efficient. The goal of being lean is to make things simpler by training ourselves to see waste and developing ways to get rid of it.

Waste is anything that does not add value. It includes things such as misinformation or miscommunication, waiting time, inefficient procedures or tools, excess inventory, and unused employee intellect.

One of the best ways we have found to get to the root of inefficiency and waste is to ask the question, "What's bugging you?" Out of this simple exercise, we have made many of our processes and systems more efficient and less wasteful.

All employees are a part of this exercise. We ask this question continually, not just once a year. This question helps us quickly get to the root of where we are wasting money and time. It helps us pinpoint steps and procedures that can make our organization more efficient.

For a guide to help your team become more innovative, view the Creativity and Innovation discussion questions in the Resources section, page 196.

INNOVATING TOGETHER

Once ideas for innovation emerge, they need teams to turn them into reality. When we select a team to innovate around an idea, we intentionally and thoughtfully discuss who should lead and drive the implementation of each idea and who else should be on the team. Leadership provides guidance and parameters and helps establish time frames and benchmarks. The team leader provides updates until the project is completed and discusses issues or concerns with leadership as they arise.

The primary role of an innovative leader is not only to innovate on his or her own, but to create an environment that brings others into the innovation process. Yes, I or others may be team leaders who guide the process, but it is next to impossible to innovate alone. *A single person can have a creative idea, but innovation almost always involves a group of people working together to bring the idea to fruition.*

● ● ● ● ● ● ● ● ● ● ● ● ● ● ● ● ●

LEADER SURVEY RESPONSES

"Great ideas come from everyone in the organization. It is important to create a culture where good ideas are heard and allowed to bubble up from the grassroots."

"Enlist the creative energy of employees to make things happen."

"You must constantly strive to be better than you were at the start of the day."

● ● ● ● ● ● ● ● ● ● ● ● ● ● ● ●

FOCUSED INNOVATION

Leaders need to focus the innovative efforts of their employees to areas that are of value to the organization. I have learned to be careful not to create an overly freewheeling environment where employees move haphazardly between projects, resulting in wasted time and resources.

Focused innovation begins with clarifying what problems exist and which new ideas to pursue. It also sets parameters around time and resources. Words like *focused* and *parameters* may sound counter-intuitive to establishing a culture of innovation, but I have found that this type of direction actually gets better results.

I have experienced how, without guidelines or directions, employees sometimes limit their energy, not wanting to overstep what they believe to be the parameters of their role. They may place tighter restrictions on themselves than I actually intend them to. On the other hand, when I give specific direction and parameters, employees are better able to focus on and work toward innovation.

On numerous occasions, I have spelled out the scope and parameters of a focused innovative effort only to have employees express surprise at how much freedom they have to act and think big. Had I not given that direction, their focus would have been too limited.

MARKETING INNOVATIONS

I believe that marketing is paramount to our success as an organization. I am continually on the lookout for cost-effective ways to get our message out to as many people as possible. I have long believed that it is not always the best product or service that wins, it's the one people know about.

While organizations must produce a quality service or product that people need or want, it does no good if nobody knows about it. Marketing is what brings the products and services to clients or customers.

When the idea of this book came into being, I immediately began thinking about the strategy for marketing it. What would the title be? Who would be the key audience? Would I follow the traditional publication model or not? What could I do now, 18 months before release, to set the groundwork for marketing? Throughout the writing process, marketing has been on my mind at every step.

Marketing is often a big part of implementing your innovation. Once the innovative project is finished, the world is going to need to know about it. They are going to need to know *what* it is and *why* it matters, and this requires marketing.

MARKETING INNOVATION EXAMPLE

For many years, we have had a variety of one-hour webinars for sale on our website. Our webinars are abbreviated content from our full-day workshops. It hit me a few years ago that one of the best ways to generate more traffic to our website, and thus more interest in our products and services, would be to offer a free webinar each month. Within a few months of starting this marketing endeavor, our monthly free webinar was the most visited page on our website – and it continues to be. I am thrilled when clients attend a workshop and indicate they first learned about us through our free webinar offering.

AUTHENTIC INNOVATION

Our focus on innovation is not always about coming up with brand new ideas. Some of the ways we have innovated have come from tweaking and adapting what others have already done or are currently doing. At times, our innovations are pieced together using information gathered from multiple sources. We often solve problems with other people's ideas, used in completely different ways.

In reality, we are not always doing things in *different* ways so much as we are doing them *our* way. We are putting our stamp on them and making them unique to us. Our training content, methods of delivery, and services are not so much original as they are authentically ours. There are other training and consulting organizations, but they are not us. Our systems, quality, values, and innovations are authentic to us.

LEADING CREATIVITY AND INNOVATION

Creativity comes easiest to those who see the world differently – to those who see the possibilities of what might be. Creativity happens when people are willing to follow their curiosity and ask questions.

Innovation comes easiest to those who are discontent with the way things are. Innovation is about working toward and beyond what is impossible, and moving from what is current to what is better. In short, innovation leads to growth and progress. Innovation is not just for profit or size, but also for knowledge, efficiency, and quality.

Leading creativity and innovation is about inspiring others to work toward growth and progress. It is about helping employees envision a different future and explore the possibilities of how to get there.

Leadership is key to fostering creativity and innovation. Leaders must act to support employees by creating the right environments and giving them the necessary resources, support, and autonomy they need. In doing so, leaders will unleash the talent of employees to work toward developing useful innovations.

ANOTHER LEADER'S INSIGHTS

PETER LOEWEN, Garden Valley Vegetable Growers

Together with his three partners, Peter leads a team of 10 employees in a commercial farming operation. Peter is an innovative leader who is always on the lookout for what's next in his industry.

Staying ahead requires us to be innovative. I'm constantly asking, "Why in the world are we growing this? Why aren't we growing that?" I'm always looking at the big picture and asking, "Why are we doing what we are doing?" Sometimes this leads us to do something different.

Years ago, my father and his brother had one of a very few farms that grew dill – they were doing something unique. The history of our farm is always in the back of my mind, and it pushes me to think beyond what we are currently doing. It has me asking what we can do now that's outside of the box, like dill was for my father and uncle.

I haven't found anything yet, but I'm still looking. I know the world is getting smaller; we can transport food all over the world. Maybe this little bit of ground we farm can grow a certain crop better than it can be grown in Asia or South America.

If you're sitting still, you're not moving anywhere. You have to keep thinking and fleshing out your ideas so that you are moving somewhere. Don't ever think that you are where you need to be. You may be in the right place for one day, but change is inevitable, and you need to be ready to move on to what's next.

Year in and year out we are exploring new potato varieties

on our farm – this process never ends. We are always look-ing for the next variety that is going to do well for us. In the last five years, we've stopped planting two potato varieties and added three new ones. When we drop a variety we've been try-ing, I don't view it as failure; instead, I see it as trial and error. I just consider it a part of the process of innovating.

On a more practical level, we are innovative with equip-ment all the time. We look at a piece of equipment that isn't working right for us and consider, "Do we go buy a new piece of equipment, or do we try to make it work?" Our first thought is always, "Let's modify what we have and make it work." We do this all the time – we are constantly adapting equipment to fit tasks that are specific to our farm.

We have to stay innovative as a farm or we won't last. I look around and often see farms that aren't innovative get bought up by the innovative ones. There's a mentality out there that leads people to say, "I farm this way because that's the way my Grandpa did." Frankly, that doesn't cut it for long, and then you are left behind. Eventually the farmers with that mentality can't pay the bills.

Being innovative requires reading and thinking. I take it upon myself to keep abreast of what's going on. I read articles related to agriculture, go to meetings, and pay attention to what's happening in the world, and then I pass that knowledge on to my partners and discuss it with them.

Innovation on our farm is not just about profit – it is also about sustainability. I think about sustainability a lot. I want this piece of ground to be here for the next generation and the one after that, so we have to care for it now and plan for the future already.

One of the things that drives me is that I feel responsible for the land that's under our care. I feel responsible because my father, and his father before him, started what I now derive my living from. So the things we are doing now have to be done *well*, not just done.

—Peter Loewen

QUESTIONS FOR REFLECTION

1. Where do you see incremental innovations in your organization?
2. As a leader, how are you fostering creativity and innovation? How are you intentionally innovating – what processes, meetings, and teams are in place?
3. What are the attitudes or processes that hinder creativity and innovation in your organization?
4. How do you personally influence and bring excitement about creativity and innovation to your organization?

To explore more questions related to creativity and innovation, be sure to review the Creativity and Innovation discussion questions in the Resources section, page 196.

9

DELEGATION

● ● ● ● ● ● ● ● ● ●

WHAT COMES NEXT

Once you have great talent, and have established a culture of productivity and innovation, what's left as an option for organizations to increase output and engagement even more? Delegation!

In various sections of this book, I refer to the importance of the *doing* – start working, keep working, and of course finish the tasks you begin. Yet the often-used adage, "work smarter, not harder," which I mentioned in the chapter on Productivity, is equally important. Delegation is about working smarter, and it's about empowering employees, which leads to increased motivation and engagement across your organization.

MY HEAD HURTS

I have already introduced you to one of my life's passions: mountain biking. While this passion has brought me joy, unfortunately it has also caused me much suffering. In late May 2015, I sustained a concussion after hitting a tree while biking.

I have had concussions before, and I've always bounced back after a few weeks. But this time my symptoms continued and even worsened over time. My ability to problem solve and my capacity to think strategically were greatly diminished. I was also dizzy all the time. To make matters worse, working on my computer exacerbated my symptoms.

For the first few weeks I tried to power through, continuing to work as much as possible despite my limitations. When the symptoms did not let up, it became clear that I needed to make a drastic change to my work style.

I slowed down. Way down. I didn't work on my computer for four straight months. I went from working 55-hour weeks to 25-hour weeks.

My concussion forced me to look at my normal work tasks and figure out what I could eliminate or delegate. I was working half time and only at partial capacity. There was no way I could do everything I had been doing before; tasks had to be removed or given to others. I was forced to delegate, but interestingly, I was also able to eliminate some tasks altogether.

ELIMINATE FIRST

Before you delegate, first eliminate. Delegation and elimination are not the same thing. When you delegate, you transfer authority or responsibility to someone else who can make decisions or complete certain tasks. When you eliminate, on the other hand, you decide that a task does not need to be delegated because no one really even needs to do it. *The worst use of time is doing something that need not be done at all.*

It is amazing how many tasks we accumulate over the years and never let go of. Most leaders have a multitude of duties they perform that are at best unnecessary, and at worst counterproductive. Many of these tasks are done for no other reason than the fact that we have always done them.

Before I sustained my concussion, I was doing a variety of unneeded tasks. I was double checking other people's work when it frankly didn't need to be checked. I was attending meetings when in fact I didn't need to be at them. I was doing things that actually didn't need to be done by anybody and thus could be eliminated.

To help determine if you can eliminate something from your workload, ask yourself:

- Why is this task needed, and how does it contribute to the functioning of our organization?
- What can I eliminate completely from my schedule? What distractions can I avoid?
- What would be the worst-case outcome if nobody did this task? If the answer is nothing, or nothing significant, then simply eliminate the task.

Always eliminate first. Never delegate something that can be eliminated, or you are just wasting someone else's time.

FOUR-HOUR WORK DAY

As a result of my concussion, I eliminated and delegated tasks because I simply had no other choice and could not continue working in the capacity I was accustomed to. Here's an interesting mental exercise for any leader to go through: How would you respond to a significant health condition that limited your ability to work?

If you had a concussion, heart attack, stroke, or other health issue that meant you could only work for four hours a day instead of your typical eight or ten, how would you manage? Most leaders would respond with, "That's impossible, I could never be effective in only four hours a day."

But consider what would happen if you had an experience similar to mine in which working your regular hours was not an option. What could you eliminate and what could you delegate? Who in your organization could do the various tasks you are responsible for?

WHY DELEGATE?

Not everything can be eliminated. Most tasks will still need to get done, whether by you or by someone else. So when delegation is optional, we must be motivated to do it for other reasons.

Effective leaders learn to delegate because transferring work to others frees up time for them to work on tasks that only they can do or that they can do best. Delegation is not merely a way to lighten your own workload; it also serves to increase the motivation and competence of those to whom you have delegated.

One of our jobs as leaders is to help people grow, and delegation assists us in doing that. Great leaders recognize *people* as an organization's most valuable resource, and they can elicit exceptional performance from their employees in part by sharing tasks.

Delegation is significantly related to employee engagement. When people are entrusted with responsibility and given the tools, support, and autonomy to complete tasks, they feel empowered. A key component of successful delegation is ensuring that employees truly feel the delegated task has become their own and that they can do it in ways that make sense to them.

Exposing employees to new tasks and challenges gives them a chance to learn, and it also shows them that their leaders trust them. When you delegate, it tells employees that you believe in their ability to perform the task, and more importantly, that you believe in them.

● ● ● ● ● ● ● ● ● ● ● ● ● ● ● ●

EMPLOYEE SURVEY RESPONSES

"If my leader wants to do the work entirely on his own, then why was I even hired?"

"I want a leader who does not tell me what to do, but rather shows me what to do."

"Leaders need to be able to lead without micromanaging. If you ask me to do something, trust that I will do it for you to the best of my ability. If you don't trust me, why am I here?"

"Nothing frustrates me more in my own workplace than when I see my administrator doing the work herself rather than delegating it."

● ● ● ● ● ● ● ● ● ● ● ● ● ● ● ●

WHAT NOT TO DELEGATE

I believe that knowing what to delegate begins with clarity about what *not* to delegate. Leaders need to focus their energy on those tasks that are most essential to the organization – those areas that would suffer if it were not for their leadership.

Ask yourself, *"What does my organization need me to do most? What do I do that is essential to the organization?"* The answers to these questions are likely the things that *only* you can do, or that you do exceedingly better than anyone else could.

For me, the answer to this question is marketing. I have always led our marketing efforts. While others could try to replicate what I do, delegating that responsibility to someone else would come with too great a risk at this stage in our organization. There are certain nuances to our marketing success that I understand, which are difficult to articulate to someone else.

Once you have named the tasks that are essential for you to do, consider whether you are spending enough time doing them. Are you giving them the effort and energy required, or are you distracted by other things on your list? *Focus only on what is important for you to do, and give the rest away.*

THE LIST

Create a list – anything that doesn't need to be done by you personally for the success of the organization is fair game. Put it all on the chopping block. If it is not crucial that you do it, and it is taking time away from what you need to do, give it up and pass it on to someone else.

Here are some questions to consider when determining what to delegate:

- What's been on your list for a long time and keeps getting moved to next week's task list?
- What tasks on the list cause you the most frustration?
- What causes you the most boredom?
- What tasks on your list are low-importance activities for you?

Start by delegating these things. Be sure to consider whether each task is something that actually can be delegated. There may be some items on your list that cause frustration or boredom, but you can't delegate them due to issues of privacy, or the fact that only you as a senior leader can do them.

Once you have delegated tasks from this list you will notice a difference. You will be freer, sharper, and more motivated. In fact, the process can be contagious; you will likely find yourself whittling down your list even further, giving you even more time to focus on what is essential.

THE SPECIFICS OF DELEGATION

Delegation happens when leaders assign the *responsibility*, *authority*, and *accountability* for a clearly defined task to someone else – a task changes hands. Responsibility relates to *how* the task will be completed. Authority refers to the *control* given to someone to act and make decisions related to the task. Accountability relates to being *answerable* for the decisions, actions, and results related to completing the task.

Once you have determined what can be delegated, consider who the tasks should be given to. Delegation works best when we give tasks to competent people who have demonstrated their abilities in areas related to the task. For those who have not yet proven themselves, start with easy tasks and increase to difficult ones gradually over time. You want people to stretch and grow, but not at the risk of significant failure.

Begin with the end in mind by clearly articulating your desired results to the employee. When people are unclear about a desired task outcome, they will often underperform rather than risk making a mistake. When clarifying task specifics, be sure to focus on the final result, not the *how to* part. Offer general suggestions on how they might proceed, but be clear that they are in charge of *how* the tasks are accomplished.

Remember to also clearly define the owner of the task. When possible, delegate the whole task, not just part of it. If you delegate just part of the task, you risk confusion about who owns it.

BE AVAILABLE

When we delegate, we must remain available as a resource. It is natural for leaders to become frustrated with employees who don't complete tasks that have been assigned to them. However, sometimes in these circumstances employees need approval to proceed or access to resources, but the leader is not available to answer requests and progress gets derailed.

We as leaders must be available to help our staff succeed. The work I do regularly takes me away from the office. When I return to the office after being gone for a few days, I know there will be a lineup of people needing approval and wanting direction from me on a variety of items that have been delegated to them.

I don't resent this. It's part of my role as a leader. My employees know that if they have questions or problems they can come and see me. *I am available.*

BARRIERS TO DELEGATION

The benefits of delegation should be clear by now, yet there are still reasons why leaders resist delegating. In my experience the most common reason relates to the old adage, "If you want something done right, do it yourself."

This actually may be true for some tasks, but that doesn't mean that those tasks are the best use of your time, or that someone else couldn't get better at them than you, given enough time and practice.

Another barrier to delegation is a leader's belief that he or she doesn't have enough time to delegate. It may feel like meeting before and during the delegation process would take more time than if you just continued to do the task yourself.

This may be the case if you are delegating a one-time task, but what about the next time a similar task needs to be done? Taking into consideration how often the task needs to be done underscores how your return on investment grows over time.

Finally, some leaders resist delegation because they believe that others can't do the job. If you buy into this belief and do not trust others, you harm yourself, your employees, and your organization.

Eventually, your organization will stop growing because there will be a bottleneck of things waiting to be done by you. Be sure to consider whether you are underestimating the abilities of your employees. Try giving employees new tasks and allowing them the freedom to complete them – they just may end up surprising you. If you truly can't trust your employees to complete tasks, you should focus much more of your energy on talent and team selection.

● ● ● ● ● ● ● ● ● ● ● ● ● ● ● ●

LEADER SURVEY RESPONSES

"Warning: micromanaging employees is a surefire way to resentfulness or sabotage!"

"A leader doesn't have to be an expert in every area; that's what team members are for."

"It is important not to do everything, but to do what is most important. If others can do it, the leader shouldn't be doing it."

● ● ● ● ● ● ● ● ● ● ● ● ● ● ● ●

DELEGATION SAVES MONEY

It's amazing how low-level tasks creep into the roles of not only leaders, but all employees. I periodically take stock of the tasks our employees are doing and find that they are working on things below their pay grade. For example, they may be working on $15 an hour tasks and being paid $25 an hour.

From a salary efficiency perspective, delegation is essential. Are the tasks you and others are doing worth the salaries the organization is paying to have them done? If not, delegate the tasks to a lower-salaried position.

Periodically take stock of the tasks you and others are doing, and assign a salary level to them. Reshuffle tasks accordingly. Fundamentally, higher-level employees should not be working on simple and routine tasks that can be done by others for a lower salary.

Having said this, it is important to note that I believe there is value in employees seeing a leader tidy the office, fix the printer, or run a simple errand – even if someone else could be paid less to do it. Helping out in these ways builds respect and serves to demonstrate leaders are not above certain tasks.

FREE TIME

Delegation done well can create time for you to work on the things that are most essential for you to invest energy in. It can also free you up to work on new and unexpected projects.

I was surprised, several months into my concussion recovery, when I went from being overwhelmed with the concern, "How am I going to accomplish everything I'm used to doing?" to actually having time for other things. I had eliminated or delegated many of my tasks in the early stages of my recovery, but as I began feeling a little better and working more hours, I filled them with new things rather than taking old tasks back.

Specifically, during my recovery period I started this book project. Ironically, my concussion forced me to eliminate and delegate tasks, and yet it created time and space for me to dedicate to this book. Interestingly, because I was still not able to work on a computer, the first three chapters were written the old fashioned way – with paper and pencil.

CHANGES IN WHAT IS MOST IMPORTANT

Over the years, the tasks our organization has needed me to do the most have changed, and I foresee changes ahead as well. When we started, I was involved in every aspect of the organization. I sat in the center of our open-concept office giving directions, providing feedback, and yes, sometimes micromanaging. When I wasn't in the office, I was meeting clients, writing content, and delivering workshops.

Eventually, I moved out of our open-concept space, which naturally changed my day-to-day role. I also began delegating the writing of new training material to people who were better at it than me. In recent years, I have reduced my role of directly managing trainers and employees to a minimum. And I have greatly reduced the number of days I personally deliver workshops.

Ten years removed from doing almost everything, my role is now primarily marketing and strategic planning related to growth, innovation, and content. Yes, I'm involved in some workshop-content creation, policy decision making, human resource management, and training, but I am primarily focused on two domains: marketing and strategic planning. That's what is most important for me to focus on right now. Yet I know this will likely change in the future.

DELEGATING WHAT WE LIKE TO DO

I really like my task of marketing. I'm good at it, and it brings me great satisfaction. Right now, I am the best person in our organization to do it. However, in the not so distant future, it is something I will likely need to delegate, as I am anticipating the volume of my writing and speaking obligations to increase.

Given the complexities and nuances involved in our marketing approach, delegating these responsibilities will be a longer-term process and will require a clear plan to nurture existing talent or bring the right talent into our organization.

Presently, I am becoming less resistant to the idea of this change. I know that it is one that will need to occur – even though I really like this task. The important learning opportunity here is that sometimes we as leaders hold on to things we enjoy longer than we should.

A leader's greatest area of strength risks becoming an organization's greatest weakness when he or she refuses to let go at the right time. All tasks need to be candidates for possible delegation. Just because we like to do something, and we're good at it, doesn't mean we should continue doing it.

DELEGATION REQUIRES TRUST

To be an effective leader, delegation is required. Delegating tasks we have handled ourselves initially can, and most often does, feel unusual. However, as organizations grow and change, so must the roles of leaders. The alternative to delegation is to keep doing everything ourselves, and this is rarely sustainable.

Delegation requires us to identify the right tasks to turn over to the right people while giving them the resources and authority to complete the task. Effective delegation saves time, increases capacity, and develops and motivates employees. *Delegation fundamentally requires trust in others. We must trust the teams we have built.*

ANOTHER LEADER'S INSIGHTS

BOB NEUFELD, Krahn Friesen Neufeld Chartered Accountants
Bob is a partner in an accounting firm with 15 staff. As a leader, he identifies delegation as essential for growing a business and keeping employees engaged.

While you have to delegate everywhere, I'm more familiar with profit-oriented businesses. That's the business I run, so I think people who delegate effectively will make more money! And while we all like to say it's about more than just money, the reality is that we wouldn't be in business if it wasn't about money to some degree. And unless you learn how to effectively delegate crucial work to other people, you are going to limit your profitability.

Delegation may not be exciting, but it is crucial. If you don't know how to delegate, you're going to run into problems. There's only so much one person can do, and everyone in business faces time pressures. We all wish for more time, and when that stress is getting to the max, we do have to take stock and consider, "What things am I doing that I don't need to do?"

What you want to delegate are meaningful tasks – tasks that other people will actually enjoy doing, and that fit within their capabilities. I don't think the reason to delegate should be, "Well, I don't like doing that," because then the questions you have to ask are, "Would anyone else like doing that? Is that task something anyone should be doing? Maybe we need to ditch that task altogether."

You want to eliminate the stuff that is pointless or not needed. Every efficient, well-run business has to do that at some point. Something you thought was necessary five, ten years ago is maybe no longer necessary. And part of that is just the advancement in technology. So it's important to sometimes stop and look and ask people, "What are we doing? Why do we even do this?" There may have been a reason for it at some point, but times have changed.

Part of what I do as a leader is develop new talent for the future. You have to develop new young people, and they're not going to grow unless you delegate things to them. You have to delegate to them things that excite them. You have to keep them satisfied, and you have to keep them motivated, so you have to put thought into what you delegate to them.

Delegating does still take time on your part because you have to be there for that person. You have to guide them, you have to answer questions, you have to review their work, or else how do you know they're doing a good job? And how does that person know? If they're supposed to develop and learn and grow, they need feedback.

As a leader, you have to think about keeping your people happy if you want them to work for you, be happy and motivated, and stay. Ultimately, as a leader, you need your people. You have to have good people, but if you don't treat them right – and that word *right* can include so many different things – why would you expect them to stay? And if they're not going to stay, that can create all sorts of problems.

I think that leaders often take their people for granted. Then they wonder later on, "Why did that person leave? How come he's quitting, or she's leaving?" Well, look in the mirror. How did you treat that person? Did you do all you could to keep them happy? It's important to keep people happy. Obviously not at all costs, but within reason.

As a leader, I can't take things for granted. I have to be

involved with staff, get to know them, find out what they like and don't like, and try to develop them. To do this, you have to delegate.

—*Bob Neufeld*

QUESTIONS FOR REFLECTION

1. Which of your current tasks could be eliminated? Why are you still doing them?
2. What shouldn't you delegate? What is the most important task for you to be doing in your organization? Are you spending enough time on this task?
3. What are some barriers that limit your desire or ability to delegate?
4. Consider the long-term implications of effective delegation. By delegating tasks, what might you have more free time to accomplish?

10

SELF-IMPROVEMENT

● ● ● ● ● ● ● ● ● ●

SHARPEN THE SAW

In my childhood, when the temperature turned colder, it was a sign that it was time to cut wood to heat our home for the winter. At least once a month during the fall and winter, my father, siblings, and I would venture out into the forest to cut wood for our woodstove.

My dad always operated the chainsaw while the rest of us split wood and loaded it into the truck. We were often faster than my dad, as he would stop to sharpen his saw frequently. Sharpening a chainsaw manually is a tedious process that took my father longer than most because he did things to perfection. Hoping to finish faster, and anticipating the warmth of our home, we would prod him to continue without the bothersome pause to sharpen the saw.

This usually only served to lengthen our day, as he would stop sharpening the saw and offer us the following lesson: "If you don't take the time throughout the day to sharpen the blades, the wood cuts much more slowly and we will be here even longer. So take a break and enjoy being in the forest while I sharpen the saw."

Years later, when I read the introduction to Habit 7 in Stephen Covey's *The 7 Habits of Highly Effective People*, the life lesson I received as a child took on even more meaning. Covey introduced me to the following parable:

> Suppose you were to come upon someone in the woods working feverishly to saw down a tree.
>
> "What are you doing?" you ask.
>
> "Can't you see?" comes the impatient reply. "I'm sawing down this tree."
>
> "You look exhausted!" you exclaim. "How long have you been at it?"
>
> "Over five hours," he returns, "and I'm beat! This is hard work."
>
> "Well, why don't you take a break for a few minutes and sharpen that saw?" you inquire. "I'm sure it would go a lot faster."
>
> "I don't have time to sharpen the saw," the man says emphatically. "I'm too busy sawing!"[1]

Covey used this parable to demonstrate the importance of becoming a better person. We are the saw, and for us to become better, we must be sharpened. We must resist the urge to always keep working toward our vision, and instead stop from time to time to work on ourselves. The lesson my father taught me as a child has meaning beyond the practical aspect of how to cut wood efficiently.

BECOMING BETTER

Becoming a better person by improving ourselves is not only good for leadership, it is also one of the most virtuous goals we can strive for as human beings. The work of improving ourselves goes by many names, including personal development, self-actualization, personal growth, and self-improvement. These terms are all similar, and they are born out of the notion that we should each strive to be the best person we can be.

Self-improvement does not just happen – like so many other insights I have written about in this book, it requires intentional, focused effort. Self-improvement requires an investment of time and energy in ourselves.

Growth rarely comes quickly or easily. Deep and lasting self-improvement is not to be found in a quick fix personal development book or podcast. *Self-improvement means moving beyond hastily assembled exterior aesthetics, and focusing instead on the internal areas – the very core of one's self.*

OUR LIFE STORY

History has always intrigued me – in particular, the stories of my heritage and those who have come before me. I have pictures of my relatives from previous generations displayed in my house. I also have various meaningful items exhibited – there is a milk jug from my uncle and grandfather's farm and a crystal dish brought over from Germany in the 1800s.

It's the stories that accompany these items that fascinate me most. When I hear tales of previous generations, I always listen intently for clues about how they thought and acted and what they believed.

I decided to return to my home community to write this chapter. I went to the place of my birth and childhood to immerse myself in the past as I ponder the present and the future. I visited old acquaintances and stopped by meaningful places.

I spent the afternoons with my grandmother in her care home. Being with her helped me focus on my life story. It helped me reflect on the meanings I ascribe to the memorable experiences that influence and shape my present day decisions and actions. I believe that the journey of self-improvement begins with understanding the story of our lives. In our personal history, we can often find solutions to current-day questions and decisions we are facing.

LIVING IN THE MOMENT

I don't believe we are meant to go through life wandering aimlessly. Yet too many of us fail to notice things. We miss the kind gesture of a stranger – or even that of a loved one. We forget to stop just for a moment to notice a majestic sunset. As winter passes, we rush in and out of heated buildings without ever throwing a snowball or riding a sled. As summer comes and goes, we fail to get on a bike or work in the garden.

Our lives are filled with a multitude of moments and wonders – of sights, sounds, and experiences that are waiting to be recognized. Yet far too often, we fail to pay attention. Instead, we are too busy thinking about our *to-do* list and *didn't-do* list, or we are stuck in the past or dreaming about the future. We are shut off from the present and fail to notice the magic of the moment.

My struggle is that I am too often stuck in the future. There have been many times when I have been looking at what's next, and missed the moment that was right in front of me. While the future I am thinking about is often exciting, I end up missing today. One of my areas of self-improvement is to work at limiting the amount of time I spend in the future. When I wander off for too long, I intentionally work at drawing myself back to the moment – living fully now, for tomorrow will come soon enough.

Others miss present moments because they are spending too much time in the past, thinking about *could haves* and *should haves*. Thinking about the past can be meaningful when we reflect on joyful memories, and it can be helpful to look for lessons learned. An interesting thing I've noticed is that when I look to the past for meaningful occasions or life lessons, I remember instances when I was actively present in the moment. I can recall it now because, at that time, I was wholly in the moment, not in the future or the past.

There is a balance between reflecting on and learning from yesterday, and not wishing for it to return. And it is okay to be excited and hopeful about the future as long as we don't let it consume the current moment.

But let us all not be numb to the daily rhythms of life that surround us. May we all strive to become more engaged with the world as it is happening now, for this is the moment that matters most.

HALFWAY THERE

I'm halfway there – slightly over, really. I'm 42. That's only 38 years to 80. I've always thought of 80 as the number that will feel as though I'll have lived a lifetime. Years seem to have sped up now – time moves faster than ever. This has made me less patient than I was before. I am not willing to waste time on negative people or meaningless activities.

My closest childhood friend died at the age of 39. That was an awakening for me. I now cherish moments and time with loved ones more than before. I have become more philosophical and nostalgic. I've even started reading obituaries. It's interesting to read obituaries and see the meaning of someone else's life summarized in a few short paragraphs.

I have begun to think more often about my life in the context of this key question: *If I were to die tomorrow, how would I want people to remember me?* The answer to this question serves as a guide for how I live my life today. It keeps me focused on living a worthy life. It helps me to consider what I am doing today to make my answer become a reality.

PLACES OF SOLITUDE

In the various places I have lived or visited frequently, I've always had my spots where I go for solitude – the special places I go by myself to sit and reflect. Solitude is important because it is only when we are alone, with the quietness of our inner thoughts, that we can find the space to truly focus. I believe these moments of quietness, away from the "pings" and "pongs" of our phones, far removed from our to-do lists, are essential for self-improvement.

My place of solitude as an adolescent was on an old country back road alongside a little creek not far from my house. I always sat facing west as the sun was setting. Even now, years later, this sacred place draws me in. I stopped by for a visit on my most recent trip home. The place is a familiar friend, even though I rarely go there now and no longer live close by. Over the years, not much has changed. The creek still runs south, the grass still whistles in the wind, and it is always quiet and peaceful.

TAKING TIME TO THINK

Solitude is really about taking time to think. Thinking allows us the space to ponder the big-picture questions and meaning of life. It's what is needed to formulate a new direction. Thinking helps generate new ways of looking at the world and inspires us to do things differently.

Thinking happens best when we slow down and are not in a rush to move on to something else. It requires us to focus on something for long enough to develop an original and meaningful idea about it. Genuine thinking moves beyond rehashing other people's ideas to focusing on finding a direction that is unique. This can't be done in five-minute bursts of time. Sometimes it can take hours or days of uninterrupted thinking time to process whatever it is that one is discerning.

The world is full of people who can *answer* questions, but who do not know how to *ask* good questions – people who can describe *how* to get things done, but who can't articulate *why* they are doing them. We have many people who can *complete* an objective but don't know how to *set* one. We have *doers*, but what we need more of is *thinkers*. We need more leaders to question the way things have been done and to contemplate the big questions. *We need leaders to spend time thinking.*

● ● ● ● ● ● ● ● ● ● ● ● ● ● ● ●

LEADER SURVEY RESPONSES

"Taking time to improve yourself demonstrates to others that there is room for development at all levels."

"Stay sharp – attend training, remain relevant, ensure you are a source of wisdom and guidance for your organization."

"Being real is important. Trying to be someone you are not will eventually lead to failure or discontent."

● ● ● ● ● ● ● ● ● ● ● ● ● ● ● ●

LEADERS DON'T ARRIVE

When I teach leadership and management principles, it is often to new or mid-level managers. Frequently, I hear comments like this: "This material is exactly what our organization needs. I just wish senior leadership was here to talk about it with us." Whether real or perceived, the message leaders send with their absence is that training and self-improvement are beneath them.

Regrettably, I have found that some leaders feel that they have arrived. They don't need additional training because they already know it all – they have been there and done that. When leaders express verbally or otherwise that they have "arrived," it not only sends a negative message to employees, it shows poor leadership.

None of us ever arrive. We don't get there. The journey of developing leadership skills is continual. I am constantly growing, learning, and changing. In the past year, as I have immersed myself in reading, thinking, and writing about these insights, I've been on a fast track of learning. My employees can name specific things I am doing differently, and better, simply as a result of my willingness to learn and change. When leaders push themselves to improve, they also build a culture of self-improvement.

Ego gets in the way of self-improvement. If you have made it this far in the book, you likely don't suffer from an overinflated ego. Someone with a big ego would have stopped at the title *The Ordinary Leader*. They would say, "This book isn't for me. I'm extraordinary, not ordinary."

Throughout the past year, I have had some interesting interactions when describing this book and my choice of title. Some people were put off by the concept of *The Ordinary Leader*. They thought too highly of themselves to be put in the category of "ordinary." But most were curious and intrigued by the title choice. They could relate to it because their egos weren't oversized.

One of the most common characteristics among all the leaders I interviewed for this book is that they are not limited by self-importance. They are unpretentious and curious, and some of them are even reluctant leaders. Leaders like this are much more prone to be successful than those with big egos, for they are willing to work at being better.

Denial is the greatest obstacle to self-awareness. Believing you have arrived is a form of denial. You can't become better if you aren't honest with yourself. Self-improvement requires genuine truthfulness with yourself. We have to be willing to be honest before we can improve.

● ● ● ● ● ● ● ● ● ● ● ● ● ● ● ●

EMPLOYEE SURVEY RESPONSES

"Big egos are part of the package when it comes to managers – unavoidable. But it is nice to hear a *bit* of genuine self-deprecation every once in a while. It's hard on the knees to have to hit the ground and chant, 'We're not worthy' all the time!"

"A leader is someone who is willing to believe that they are not the be-all, end-all, and do-all. They are striving to be better."

● ● ● ● ● ● ● ● ● ● ● ● ● ● ● ●

READING FOR IMPROVEMENT

A common theme among successful (and frankly, interesting) people I know is that they read. They read the news, their industry's articles, and leadership and how-to books. They read to be informed and to improve themselves, not just to increase their knowledge.

I believe there is no better way to expand the mind than by reading. In recent years, I have watched my children bemoan being *required* to read a certain book for school, only to hear them reference an insight from it weeks later. This never changes. Throughout the spectrum of life, some of our best opportunities for self-improvement come from immersing ourselves in other people's thoughts.

I've provided a list of some of my favorite leadership books on page 177.

MEETING PEOPLE WHERE THEY ARE

One of the growth areas I have identified for myself is the ability to adapt to others and meet them where they are. Historically, I have expected people to adapt to me and meet me where I am. This hasn't always worked, and I realize now that I need to be more flexible in how I engage with various employees.

I have a strong personality, and I am prone to asserting my will and giving direction for my desired results. But I am learning to be willing to compromise and meet people where they are. I am more open to respecting and implementing another individual's point of view rather than forcing my own.

Everything we are trying to accomplish as an organization involves other people, and even though I have authority, people don't always have to agree with me. Letting employees know that I care about their ideas helps me nurture relationships while at the same time achieving desired results.

AUTHENTIC LEADERSHIP

Many positive adjectives can precede the word leadership – servant leadership, empathetic leadership, and compassionate leadership to name a few. The adjective I like the most is *authentic*. For me, authenticity ties together so many of the words used to describe good leadership. Being authentic is about expressing yourself congruently – the person others see is who you really are. *Authenticity means being genuine and true to who you are. You are not a pretender or an imitation of someone else. You don't exaggerate or minimize who you are or what you believe in.*

This is my answer to the question I asked earlier in the chapter: *If I were to die tomorrow, how would I want people to remember me?* I hope that people see me as authentic. I may not be the most empathetic leader, and I don't think servant leadership describes me, but I do hope people see me as an authentic leader. I hope they see that I am who I say I am. I'm no different at home than I am at work. There is congruency between what I think and what I say.

While it's not an exhaustive list, these are some of the key components of authenticity I identify with and strive for:

- **Genuineness**: This is the most important component of authenticity. Authentic leaders don't communicate using a hidden agenda. They are honest and straightforward in their interactions with others, regardless of the circumstances.
- **Integrity**: Authentic leaders walk the talk and always keep their word. They have an ethical core, and they are honest, trustworthy, and believable. Regardless of who is watching (or if nobody is watching at all), they will do the right thing when faced with difficult dilemmas.
- **Compassion**: Authentic leaders value the welfare of employees and are not afraid to demonstrate kindness and concern. Compassionate leaders treat people at work as they would like to be treated themselves.

- **Vulnerability**: Authentic leaders are not afraid to be open and honest about their weaknesses. They admit that they are not perfect and that there are things they don't know. Vulnerability also means not being afraid to show emotions or connect with employees on a human level.

Authenticity is the alignment of what we say with what we do – consistently. *Authenticity does not have an on-off switch – we are either authentic all the time or not at all.*

FOCUS ON INTEGRITY

A key theme found in the qualitative data of the employee survey was that a leader's integrity matters greatly to employees. Integrity was the most mentioned principle that wasn't in the list of 10 that respondents could choose from. Employees said things like:

"Integrity is essential. If there is no integrity, there is nothing."

"I don't want to be associated with an organization that does not have integrity."

"Integrity is key. If leaders don't have it, the whole organization suffers."

"You need to have integrity as a leader. Otherwise, why would your team have any faith in you?"

"Integrity is a must. Employees quickly spot the hypocrisy in leader's statements when they don't line up with how that leader behaves toward others."

For all of us, our integrity is often at risk in small ways. The first slip goes unnoticed – you know you've done something wrong but others don't. We justify letting ourselves compromise our integrity *just this once.* But it's a slippery slope – as soon as we compromise once, it's easier to do so again.

We must be vigilant in protecting our integrity. When we're facing questionable decisions, we always need to consider how our actions will impact our integrity.

BE BETTER

Self-improvement is not possible if we don't honestly look at our lives and consider who we are and what makes us tick.

I encourage you to spend time considering life's big questions:

- Am I happy with who I am and who I'm becoming?
- Am I fulfilled with how I am contributing to the world?
- Am I living a meaningful life?

I also encourage you to consider these important leadership questions:

- What perceptions do my employees have of me as a leader?
- Am I an authentic leader?
- Do I demonstrate that I care for my employees?
- Do my employees trust me?

Asking ourselves these types of questions helps us face the truth. It helps us to re-evaluate and focus in on what is important.

Slowing down and disengaging from the busyness of our lives is essential for reflection, renewal, and improvement. *Take the time to be better.*

ANOTHER LEADER'S INSIGHTS

LYNDA MONK, Creative Wellness
Lynda is the owner of a company through which she provides coaching and speaking services. She is an author and leader in the field of wellness and creativity, and she believes that self-improvement is essential for effective leadership.

As long as we're continuing to grow, to learn something new about ourselves, and to adapt to that learning, we're in the lane of self-improvement.

When I think of leaders who continually strive to know themselves and grow themselves – in my experience, they're the people who make the greatest impact. They tend to be the leaders whom other people can relate to, trust, and want to work alongside of, and they are generally just a lot more fun and inspiring to be around.

Other people decide whether we are leaders or not. Obviously you might have a title that says you're a leader, but in terms of who we are and how we impact people, we don't really decide that. The proof is in whether or not other people consider us to be leaders. Do they find us inspiring and impactful? Do they want to learn something from us? Do they want to know us, be with us, and listen to what we have to say? Do they feel we really care about what they have to say and contribute?

I deeply believe that the more I am willing to invest in my own personal improvement, the better I'm able to support others with that journey. The more deeply we are prepared to improve ourselves, the more we become catalysts to help other people do the same.

I do a lot of intentional things for my own growth and

improvement. The more intention we bring to something, the more transformative it can be. A lot of times as leaders, our attention is divided between all kinds of things, and so bringing our attention to self-improvement is a real act of will.

Self-improvement can often feel like a solitary path in which we step away, and we're quiet and reflective. That's true for me. I spend a lot of time journaling in particular; expressive and reflective writing has been a key tool for my own personal growth. I sometimes take a half day or a couple of days and go away somewhere where I can really unplug and step away from all the devices and distractions that can be in our midst. My purpose is to pause and say, "Who am I now? Where am I at? What's working? What needs to shift? How am I feeling?"

I believe that all self-improvement, in some way, is in service of the relationships I have with myself, with others, and with the world we live in. We're never just in isolation; there's always a sense of interconnectedness. When I'm in that quiet space, I'm often considering who I am and how I'm doing in relationship with someone or something else – my children, partner, clients, colleagues, business, and so forth.

If I ever wrote a book about leadership, it would include something on *decent* leadership. There's a lot to be said about being a decent, kind, evolving, and caring leader. People who I see succeeding, enjoying what they do, contributing to the people they work with – they're good people, and they're down to earth as well. They're in there, they're doing the work, and they're trying to help other people do the work.

I also resonate with the term *conscious leadership* – people who are willing to be awake; people who are willing to look at interconnectedness. I want to strive to be a conscious leader. I want to pay attention to the connections between people and events. I want to be aware, I want to be awake, I want to evolve, and I want to make a contribution.

Showing up to be the best version of ourselves we can be and reach our full potential – that changes everything. That changes how we lead and how we regard ourselves and others. The more vulnerable we are, the more authentic and real we are, and the more accessible we are to others.

—*Lynda Monk*

QUESTIONS FOR REFLECTION

1. What do you do to intentionally "sharpen your saw?"
2. How do you make time for solitude and thinking? How can you make this an essential priority, not just something to do "if I have time?"
3. Does your leadership reflect your authentic self? Where it does not, how can you ensure your actions match your words and thoughts?

CONCLUSION

● ● ● ● ● ● ● ● ● ●

CONNECTIONS

By now it should be clear that the leadership insights presented in this book do not stand alone, isolated from one another. The connections are endless. One leader who took part in the survey noted the connections in this way:

> I believe all 10 principles you have identified are critical for success as a leader. Each one impacts the other. For example, passion is the bedrock of what I do as a leader. Self-awareness is critical for ensuring I am working with my strengths and talents and helping others to do the same. A clear vision leads to how I delegate and prioritize. I see all of these things as a weave of elements that make the whole of a successful leader and a thriving organization, regardless of its size.

OUR APPROACH TO LEADERSHIP

In my introduction, I noted that if you identify as a leader, it is important for you to be able to articulate your personal approach to leadership. I also encouraged you to think about how the insights in this book might influence your approach.

Your leadership philosophy is very personal, just as my approach to leadership is mine alone. There is no precise blueprint to replicate from this book, or from any other. Of course we can and should learn from others as we shape our own view of leadership. In reality there are as many leadership approaches as there are leaders.

You've made the decision to lead. Yes, the decision. If you identify as a leader, that is because you have chosen to. As a leader, I believe it is paramount that you understand and can express your approach to leadership. I hope this book has helped you be better able to do so.

PARTING THOUGHTS

My parting thoughts are important. I toiled over the exact wording for hours – I wanted to get them right. Yes, they are for you the reader, but they are also for my children and other loved ones in my life – my nieces, my nephews, and my friends' children; those on the cusp of making important choices.

No matter who or what is tugging you one way or the other, it is you who is in charge of your life. You're it – the answers to the questions at hand can and should be provided by you. Don't stand around waiting for someone to tell you which way to go or to give you permission – forge ahead on your own accord. Yes, seek advice from those you respect, but know that the final decision rests with you.

Life's decisions are yours and yours alone. You don't need to seek approval for how you live life or what you do with it. Your life need not follow any path other than that of your choosing. You are free to choose. There is no consent needed.

How you decide to use that freedom is up to you. So be an active participant.

Don't just let things stay the same. Be willing to take risks and step into the unknown. Those who play it safe are the ones who usually have the smallest dreams. Those who were first to cross oceans and stand atop mountains were those who were courageous, independent, and in control of their lives.

So dream big and dream loud, with just a little bit of audaciousness and an edge. Life continually asks, "What's next? What do you want?" Use your freedom to answer these questions. *Assert your voice and take the leap!*

SURVEY RESPONSES

● ● ● ● ● ● ● ● ● ●

I was amazed by the number of survey respondents who took the time to thoughtfully provide their opinions and perspectives in writing. Some of these responses have been placed throughout the book. What follows are additional responses. There were far too many to include them all, so I list only a brief sample of the ones we received.

LEADER SURVEY RESPONSES

"I must be able to follow as well as lead."

"You can't lead if you don't have relationships. Knowing your employees is crucial."

"When I think of the best leaders who have touched my life and helped me, these leaders seemed to know and accept who I was, while encouraging me to do my best. They were professional, respectful, and engaged, which instilled in me the confidence to reach a little higher and do a little better."

"A great leader inspires rather than directs. That is the difference between a boss and a leader."

"I am here to motivate, provide resources, cheer employees on, and celebrate the good. And I am here to pick up the pieces and help us regroup if things don't go as planned."

"Leadership is not the person at the front telling a passive crowd what to do."

"People want their leaders to listen. Leaders don't have to agree with what's being said by employees, but they do need to listen and seek to understand. People want to be understood at two levels: intellectual and emotional. At the intellectual level, people want their leaders to understand what they are saying. At the emotional level, people want their leaders to understand what they are feeling."

"I am guided by two principles: 'People remember how you made them feel,' and 'Treat others the way you want to be treated.'"

"And fun! You have to have fun in the workplace."

"Perhaps the best skill I have honed is becoming a borrower. I try to integrate the leadership qualities I have admired and I've seen them work for both me and my staff. On the other hand, I try to stay away from characteristics that have led to poor results."

"To be an effective leader, you must first realize that leadership is a behavior, not a position."

"I strongly believe in being a leader instead of a boss, so I try to lead rather than rule."

"Know when to stop talking and start listening. You can only see a situation through your eyes and based on your own experiences and knowledge. That puts on blinders. Hear what your staff is trying to tell you."

"Follow the golden rule: Never treat employees in a way you wouldn't want to be treated."

"Know when to say, 'I'm sorry. I was wrong.' Employees cannot function if they are afraid of making mistakes. It is imperative to set the example that no one should cling to an illusion of perfection."

"I work hard to ensure that everyone is treated equally – no matter where you fall on the organizational chart, everyone's job is important for the success of the company."

"Possessing strong self-confidence allows me to be okay with being wrong about something and not become defensive. It allows me to be open to other people's ideas without feeling threatened."

"Lots of leaders talk about people being our most important asset, but then do and say things that are not congruent."

"Well-trained and committed employees don't need the boss watching and commenting on all they do."

"I can't stress enough that not talking to employees and not providing updates will eat away at your organization. Mistrust will lead to resentment, which will pull a once highly productive organization down."

"People don't care how much you know until they know how much you care."

EMPLOYEE SURVEY RESPONSES

"Occasionally leaders need to be followers."

"Some observations about things that don't work in leadership:

- Lack of planning: chaos breeds disrespect and blame.
- Dishonesty: white lies and omissions count.
- Micromanaging: it's cloaked disrespect.
- Not backing your team: sometimes even when they are dead wrong.
- Too many secrets held by too few: elitism is also disrespect."

"Be the lighthouse that lets me engage the heavy seas and feel safe enough to do so."

"At my organization I don't see leaders, only bosses who give orders and instructions."

"The best way to lead is by example. Unfortunately, there are few true leaders in my organization who should be followed. If I followed my leader's example, I would

- not return calls or emails,
- dodge important issues,
- not do things in a timely manner,
- take time off when things are stressful, and
- react in inappropriate ways."

"Leaders should take the time to have at least a passing knowledge of what each of their employees do on a regular basis."

"The difference between leaders and managers: leaders lead thinkers. Thinkers follow those they have chosen to follow; it requires active participation. Managers lead followers – those who are unwilling or unable to think for themselves. This process requires little to no participation."

"Leaders must be team players because no one likes a 'lord it over' dictator."

"I want leaders to value my ability to help achieve the organization's goals and not just pay lip service to my strengths."

"The most successful leaders I have seen are able to identify and connect with their staff."

"Leaders need to be able to stand up for staff when appropriate – they need to have their employees' backs."

"Successful leaders know that they would never have achieved their own success without the help of those around them."

"Leaders need the ability to understand what is being said (and sometimes, not said) by employees."

"In my government department, systems change at a snail's pace. For many, this justifies not trying to change or improve things because in effect 'it is too difficult.' I wish my leaders had more of a 'can do' attitude."

"Leaders need to be able to take time to have fun and realize that staff are people."

BOOK RECOMMENDATIONS

● ● ● ● ● ● ● ● ● ●

MY TOP 10 LEADERSHIP BOOKS

Limiting my number of book recommendations to a list of 10 has been an interesting exercise. I could add more to the list, but these are the ones that have inspired me most to think differently and grow as a leader.

I have read these books over the past decade. It's important to note that my state of mind, or issues I was struggling with while reading, greatly affected my willingness to be impacted by them. These books addressed important issues for me right when I needed guidance.

Big Magic: Creative Living Beyond Fear by Elizabeth Gilbert (Riverhead Books, 2015)

Beautifully written. Yes, I just used the word *beautiful* to describe a book about leadership. I was hooked after the first few paragraphs, and I couldn't put it down until it was finished. This book will get your creative juices flowing, and you will be primed for innovation. If not now, eventually you *need* to read this book! The language, style, concepts – everything about it is simply beautiful.

*And you have treasures hidden within you – extraordinary trea-
sures – and so do I, and so does everyone around us. And bringing those treasures to light takes work and faith and focus and
courage and hours of devotion, and the clock is ticking, and the
world is spinning, and we simply do not have time anymore to
think so small* (page 27).

Delivering Happiness: A Path to Profits, Passion, and Purpose by
Tony Hsieh (Business Plus, 2010)

This is a story about building and then sustaining a unique organization. Hsieh shows how to create a corporate culture that values
people and relationships. This book is inspiring for those interested in
providing customer service at a very high level. It is written from a very
personal viewpoint by the founder and CEO of Zappos.

No matter what your past has been, you have a spotless future
(page 227).

Drive: The Surprising Truth About What Motivates Us by Daniel H.
Pink (Riverhead Books, 2009)

This book challenges assumptions about motivation and provides
a new lens through which to view employee engagement. Practical
techniques for increasing motivation are provided throughout. The
book is well researched and the writing style makes it easy to understand the concepts presented.

*Here's something you can do to keep yourself motivated. At the
end of each day, ask yourself whether you were better today
than you were yesterday. Did you do more? Did you do it well?*
(page 155).

Pour Your Heart Into It: How Starbucks Built a Company One Cup at a Time by Howard Schultz and Dori Jones Yang (Hyperion, 1997)

I love stories about building something special, and this is one of the best stories out there. From beginning to end, there are meaningful observations about how decisions were made at Starbucks during its meteoric growth. If you are working at scaling your organization, this book will be helpful in your planning. If you do read it, you will soon want to read the follow-up book, *Onward: How Starbucks Fought for Its Life Without Losing Its Soul.* This book reads like a novel: enjoyable, accessible, and applicable to a wide audience.

> *In this ever-changing society, the most powerful and enduring brands are built from the heart. They are real and sustainable. Their foundations are stronger because they are built with the strength of the human spirit, not an ad campaign. The companies that are lasting are those that are authentic* (page 248).

Tap Dancing to Work: Warren Buffett on Practically Everything, 1966-2012 by Carol J. Loomis (Portfolio, 2013)

Buffett is so much more than an investor. He is also a leader and an entrepreneur. His unique, genuine, and sometimes humorous insights are found throughout these pages. This book is one of the longest listed here, but it is easy to read.

> *You never know who's swimming naked until the tide goes out* (page 161).

The Advantage: Why Organizational Health Trumps Everything Else in Business by Patrick Lencioni (Jossey-Bass, 2012)

This book provides practical guidance for how to build and sustain organizational health. In my view, this is the most actionable book on this list. The writing style is very accessible and the content is laid out in such a way that you can quickly refer back to it when you need to.

> *There is just no escaping the fact that the single biggest factor determining whether an organization is going to get healthier – or not – is the genuine commitment and active involvement of the person in charge... At every step in the process, the leader must be out front, not as a cheerleader or a figurehead, but as an active, tenacious driver* (page 190).

The Motivation Manifesto: 9 Declarations to Claim Your Personal Power by Brendon Burchard (Hay House, 2014)

I usually run fast and far from self-help books, but this one is different. If you need some help with motivation, this is a great place to start. The book's style is rich and complex, and it requires time to fully integrate and appreciate each sentence.

> *Great men and women don't give a damn if anyone approves. They rarely seek permission from the world, because they know that the masses bound by mediocrity will never approve of anything that breaks convention or smacks of boldness and magic* (page 145).

The Truth About Leadership: The No-Fads, Heart-of-the-Matter Facts You Need to Know by James M. Kouzes & Barry Z. Posner (Jossey-Bass, 2010)

If I were teaching a university course in leadership, this would be one of the books I would require students to read. The book provides a review of the essential elements of leadership and is laid out in a practical, easy-to-read style that flows easily from one chapter to the next.

There seems to be this myth about leadership that what you are supposed to do is ascend the mountain, gain enlightenment, descend with the tablets, and then proclaim the truth to your followers. Nothing could be more damaging to the work of a leader (page 42).

The War of Art: Break Through the Blocks and Win Your Inner Creative Battles by Steven Pressfield (Black Irish Entertainment LLC, 2002)

This is a different kind of book than you would normally expect to find on a list of leadership books, but it's simply an amazingly insightful and masterfully crafted piece of work. If you are currently procrastinating on starting something, this book will give you the boost you need. Though it is small in size, it requires slow, focused attention to fully appreciate.

Resistance is faster than a speeding bullet, more powerful than a locomotive, harder to kick than crack cocaine. We're not alone if we've been mowed down by Resistance; millions of good men and women have bitten the dust before us. And here's the biggest bitch: We don't even know what hit us (from the Introduction).

Tribes: We Need You to Lead Us by Seth Godin (Portfolio, 2008)

Godin is a master wordsmith who, in a just a few short sentences, will have you thinking about leadership in different ways than you ever have before. For those of you with no time to read, this is an accessible book and a quick read – it's the shortest book on this list.

Part of leadership (a big part of it, actually) is the ability to stick with the dream for a long time. Long enough that the critics realize that you're going to get there one way or another... so they follow (page 132).

RESOURCES

● ● ● ● ● ● ● ● ● ● ●

The resources in this section provide more detailed guidance and examples for putting the ideas presented in this book into action. Each has been mentioned in one of the preceding chapters. Along with each resource, I note the chapter to which it is related so you can go back and re-read those sections you found most helpful. The topics highlighted here follow the same order in which they were referenced in this book. Choose an area you would like to explore more, and go directly there.

EMPLOYEE ENGAGEMENT ASSESSMENT
Referenced in Chapter 1, page 19.

The Employee Engagement Assessment tool is designed to gather focused feedback on issues that affect employee engagement. Leaders can use this information to facilitate thoughtful and proactive discussions related to findings.

Instructions
Review the statements below and rate each statement on a scale of 1 to 10. A 10 indicates you strongly agree with the statement; a 1 indicates you strongly disagree with the statement.

___ 1. Most days I am happy and satisfied with the work I do.
___ 2. I have freedom to choose how best to accomplish my work.
___ 3. I have a good understanding of the mission and vision of the organization.
___ 4. I can see a link between my work and the organization's mission and vision.
___ 5. It's important to me that the quality of my work is high.
___ 6. I have the information, or access to information, that I need to do my work.
___ 7. I am paid fairly for the work I do.
___ 8. My job provides me with a sense of purpose and meaning.
___ 9. My job makes good use of my skills and abilities.
___ 10. I feel I have the tools and resources I need to do my work.
___ 11. I feel valued for the work I do.
___ 12. I am proud to work at my organization.
___ 13. I feel encouraged to continually develop my skills.
___ 14. The work I do is interesting and challenges me.
___ 15. I am encouraged to try things in new ways.

Interpreting Results

Responses to questions that range from 1 to 5 should be viewed with concern, particularly when that result is seen in more than one survey. Organizational leaders should focus their attention on resolving these issues quickly. Responses ranging from 6 to 7 may indicate an area that should be watched or given secondary attention. Responses ranging from 8 to 10 should be celebrated.

CONFLICT RESOLUTION AND RESPECTFUL WORKPLACE GUIDELINES

Referenced in Chapter 6, page 96.

CTRI and ACHIEVE use the guidelines below internally to resolve conflict and develop a respectful workplace. We review this document with all new staff as part of the orientation process.

Conflict Resolution

Conflict is unavoidable. It is inherent within all organizations and groups. Conflict is not the same as disrespect, although people may behave disrespectfully within conflict. There are many sources of conflict, including disagreements, personality clashes, and differences of opinion. When workers share a high level of trust and have strong communication skills, conflicts are usually easily navigated and resolved. However, minor conflicts can quickly escalate when there is a breach of trust, a miscommunication or misinterpretation of words or actions, or a lack of interpersonal or problem-solving skills.

Respectful Workplace

Disrespect is any type of behavior that causes offense to someone else. This might include putting others down, abusing them verbally, avoiding or ignoring them, bullying them, and using negative body language. Respect, on the other hand, is when people treat each other with consideration and empathy. When people respect each other they safeguard the dignity of their coworkers. Respect encompasses more than just showing restraint and putting up with certain people or behaviors. Respect also entails welcoming differences and recognizing that they contribute to a vibrant workplace.

Focus on Impact

When it comes to issues of respect and conflict, it is the impact of our actions that matters, not our intentions. An individual may have no intent to be disrespectful, but if he or she is perceived as disrespectful, then the behavior is disrespectful. If our intent was not malicious but the effect was negative, we must acknowledge, apologize for, and change our behavior, even when we meant no harm.

Approaching Disrespect and Conflict

When tensions around disrespect or conflict arise in the workplace, let the following principles guide you:

Before doing anything, remember:

1. Most people do not act with poor intentions, so when you are feeling badly about something someone has done or said, assume that they probably did not mean to hurt you.
2. Most people want to be approached directly when someone else has a concern about something they have done or said.
3. Email and social media are very poor ways to address disrespect and conflict. They typically only escalate the situation. Address issues in person, or if that is not possible, over the phone.

Starting a conversation:

1. Most people prefer to be asked about their actions first rather than being told how their actions did not work. So start with a question about what was behind a certain action, for example, "I'm curious about what you meant when you said…"
2. Listen – try to understand.
3. If necessary, share how a person's actions affected you, as well as what you would prefer that person to have said.

Always remember:

1. Ask if there would be a better time to talk.
2. Suggest bringing in another person to help the conversation (peer or manager).
3. Approach your team leader for confidential coaching on how to handle the situation. Note that a manager will not generally convey a message on your behalf. Instead, they will help you figure out what to say or do, or they will hold a joint meeting to help everyone talk.

MISSION, BELIEFS, VISION, AND CORE VALUES
Referenced in Chapter 3, page 50, and Chapter 6, page 96.

Our mission, beliefs, vision, and core values are referenced regularly in our planning, meetings, and discussions at work. This information is also displayed on various walls throughout our offices.

ACHIEVE Centre for Leadership & Workplace Performance and the Crisis & Trauma Resource Institute

Mission
To provide exceptional training and resources to better lives.

Beliefs
We believe access to knowledge and skill development changes individual lives, communities, and organizations; and we believe that people should be able to like where they work.

Vision
At CTRI we envision a future where everyone has access to *high quality* mental health, counseling, and violence-prevention resources. At ACHIEVE we envision a future where everyone has access to *high quality* leadership and workplace development resources. We aspire to be the *most trusted, accessible,* and *widely known* provider of these resources.

Core Values

- **Embody**: We practice what we teach.
- **Engaged**: We care about being here.
- **Exceptional**: We have a diverse skill set and each of us excels at something.
- **Productive**: We work hard and get things done.
- **Receptive**: We are open to feedback and change.

ORGANIZATIONAL HEALTH ASSESSMENT
Referenced in Chapter 6, page 98.

The Organizational Health Assessment tool assists administrators in understanding organizational and team health. This tool is useful for generating engaging and proactive discussions within teams about what is or is not going well.

Instructions

Review the statements below and rate each statement on a scale of 1 to 10. A 10 indicates you strongly agree with the statement; a 1 indicates you strongly disagree with the statement.

_____ 1. People enjoy spending time with their coworkers.

_____ 2. Grievances and/or harassment claims are rare.

_____ 3. Problems and issues are discussed openly.

_____ 4. I feel like people at work care about my well-being.

_____ 5. People tell the truth because they will be heard.

_____ 6. Team members clearly understand their role and others' roles in the organization.

_____ 7. There is a strong sense of trust at all levels in the organization.

_____ 8. There is regular dialogue about how to work more effectively together.

_____ 9. Disrespect and conflict are minimal, and if they arise, they are managed quickly.

_____ 10. Employees rarely participate in gossip and petty talk.

_____ 11. I am treated with fairness and respect.

_____ 12. Information is shared openly between employees and management.

_____ 13. I have positive relationships with my coworkers and my leaders.

_____ 14. When someone makes a mistake, they do not fear criticism and punishment.

_____ 15. I feel like I am connected to others and that I belong here.

Interpreting Results

Responses to questions that range from 1 to 5 should be viewed with concern, particularly when that result is seen in more than one survey. Organizational leaders should focus their attention on resolving these issues quickly. Responses ranging from 6 to 7 may indicate an area that should be watched or given secondary attention. Responses ranging from 8 to 10 should be celebrated.

LEADERSHIP STRENGTHS AND WEAKNESSES ASSESSMENT

Referenced in Chapter 4, page 63 and page 70.

The Leadership Strengths and Weaknesses Assessment tool is designed to generate thoughtful and honest discussions around a leader's strengths and weaknesses. The facilitator asks participants to reflect and write responses to questions listed in the assessment. This is followed by sharing and discussing those responses. Discussion is focused on working to improve strengths (our greatest potential for growth) and to mitigate and manage weaknesses that get in the way of performance.

Definitions

Relational Strengths and Weaknesses: How we interact with our peers and those we manage. This includes how we demonstrate skills like respect, empathy, listening, communication, and supportiveness.

Operational Strengths and Weaknesses: How competent we are in the practical aspects of managing our organization. This is related to things such as strategic planning, finance, human resources, and marketing.

Use the questions below to analyze your strengths and weaknesses:

Relational Strengths and Weaknesses Questions

1. What interactions with staff bring you the most satisfaction?
2. What interactions with staff are you most prone to avoid?
3. What interactions or situations with staff cause them to distance themselves from you?
4. What is the most common positive feedback you receive?
5. What is the most common negative feedback you receive?
6. What do people at work like about you?
7. What do people at work dislike about you?

8. If you no longer worked in your organization, what would your team miss about you?

Operational Strengths and Weaknesses Questions

1. What are the things you excel at in your current role?
2. What evidence do you have to support the notion that you excel at these things?
3. What are the things you defer or hand off to others to do?
4. What are the things you don't do well in your current role?
5. What is the most common positive feedback you receive?
6. What is the most common negative feedback you receive?
7. If you no longer worked in your organization what would your team miss about your work?

Discussion Questions

1. What surprised you or made you think as you worked through the assessment?
2. How could you better use your areas of greatest strength?
3. What are ways you can better mitigate areas of weakness?
4. How do other team members' strengths cover for your weaknesses?
5. How is the distinction between operational and relational strengths and weaknesses helpful?

SAMPLE JOB POSTING
Referenced in Chapter 5, page 79 and page 80.

In this example of one of our typical job postings, note how the qualifications relate to both the tasks and the organizational culture. Also note the question related to cultural fit that we ask applicants to respond to in writing found under "To Apply."

Social Media and Marketing Coordinator
The Crisis and Trauma Resource Institute (www.ctrinstitute.com) requires a full-time person to work in the area of social media and email marketing. This person will begin working _____ (there is room to be flexible on start date). CTRI provides training and resources in the areas of mental health, counseling, and violence prevention.

Key Duties
- Placing ads and blog posts on social media platforms
- Creating ads for Facebook and LinkedIn
- Working with Google ads
- Designing and sending email marketing campaigns
- Organizing and maintaining email data
- Assessing the success of various marketing campaigns
- Proofing and editing material

While competency in all areas is not required, candidates should have the aptitude to learn new tasks in these areas quickly.

Qualifications
- Personable and friendly, fun and grounded
- Likes people and enjoys speaking with others
- Can accept feedback and make changes with minimal defensiveness

- Exceptional contributor to team environment
- Demonstrates continuous self-improvement
- Excellent computer skills and aptitude to learn new programs quickly
- Excellent writing skills
- Self-motivated and able to work independently
- Ability to handle and prioritize multiple tasks
- Strong time and organizational management skills
- Pays attention to detail
- Knowledge of Facebook, LinkedIn, and Twitter as marketing tools

Wage/Benefits
- Will vary depending on qualifications and experience
- Four weeks of paid vacation/personal days/Christmas holidays
- Extended benefits after three months of employment

To Apply

Please send the following in one attachment: Résumé, cover letter, three work/school related references and a response to the following questions:

1. What do you do to contribute to a healthy, vibrant work culture?
2. Please describe your understanding of the work CTRI does and how the position of Social Media and Marketing Coordinator helps in fulfilling this mandate.

Closing and Interviews

Applications will be accepted until Wednesday, _____ at noon. Successful applicants will be contacted by phone on _____ to set up a brief video interview. Final follow-up interviews will be the week of _____.

SAMPLE INTERVIEW QUESTIONS
Referenced in Chapter 5, page 81.

This is a sample of the types of questions we typically ask candidates. These questions are intended to help us assess fit for both culture and tasks. In addition to these questions, we include some standard questions like, "Tell us about yourself," and questions specific to each job description.

1. What would your past and present coworkers say about you if I asked them to describe you?
2. How would you describe your relationships with your past and present coworkers? Do you have friends at work?
3. Why did you apply for this position? *Possible follow-up*: Why did you leave your last job? Why do you want to leave your current job? How selective is your job hunt? Did you apply to just this specific job or to many others?
4. What kinds of activities or roles come easily for you? What do you learn quickly?
5. What activities and roles bring you a sense of satisfaction? What do you look forward to doing? What leads you to feel satisfied at the end of a day?
6. What annoys you at work? What makes you happy at work?
7. Tell us about a time when you received some feedback that was hard for you to hear. How did you respond to that feedback?
8. Tell us about a time when someone said or did something that bothered you. What did you do in response?
9. What makes you laugh? (When will we hear you laugh?)
10. Please provide examples of how you align with our core values.

CREATIVITY AND INNOVATION DISCUSSION QUESTIONS
Referenced in Chapter 8, page 132 and page 139.

Developing creative ideas and implementing useful innovations are easier when teams have intentional and thoughtful conversations related to the four subject areas below. Here are questions to use that will help focus discussion on these areas. When the term *client* is used, it could also refer to a customer, a vendor, or an internal person or department.

What Problems Do People Have?
These questions are intended to identify current or future clients' problems:

1. What are the common problems clients are identifying?
2. What are frustrations or pain points we observe clients experiencing?
3. If you were a client, what would you see as a problem?

What Do People Want?
These questions are intended to identify what services or products clients want:

1. What are clients asking for that we are not providing?
2. If you were a client, what new or different things would you want our organization to do?
3. How can we provide what clients value and want the most? How can we provide those things in different ways?

What Do People Need?
These questions are intended to identify what services or products clients need, including those things they may not even know they need:

1. What possible needs do our clients have that we are not offering a solution for?
2. What future trends will impact our clients' needs?
3. How can we provide our services or products in different ways that clients may value?

What's Bugging You?

This section is intended to help organizations become less wasteful and more efficient. How, and in what areas, are you being bugged? Do you think there is waste in any of the following categories?

1. Time spent searching for items or information
2. Misinformation or miscommunication
3. Waiting time
4. Inefficient procedures or tools
5. Excess inventory
6. Unused employee intellect
7. Over-production
8. Over-processing
9. Transportation
10. Defects and mistakes

REFERENCES

●●●●●●●●●●

Introduction

1. Randy Grieser. "Motivation Matters Most." ACHIEVE Centre for Leadership & Workplace Performance, 2016, http://achievecentre .com/motivation.

Chapter 1

1. "State of the Global Workplace." Gallup Inc., 2013, http://www.securex .be/export/sites/default/.content/download-gallery/nl/brochures/ Gallup-state-of-the-GlobalWorkplaceReport_20131.pdf, 12.
2. "What Drives Employee Engagement and Why It Matters." Dale Carnegie & Associates Inc., 2012, https://www.dalecarnegie.com/ assets/1/7/driveengagement_101612_wp.pdf, 2.
3. Daniel H. Pink, *Drive: The Surprising Truth About What Motivates Us* (New York: Riverhead Books, 2009), 71.

Chapter 2

1. Simon Sinek, *Start With Why: How Great Leaders Inspire Everyone To Take Action* (New York: Portfolio, 2009), 39.
2. Marcus Buckingham and Donald O. Clifton, *Now, Discover Your Strengths* (New York: The Free Press, 2001), 19.

Chapter 5

1. "Future Proof Plans: 12th Annual Global CEO Survey." PricewaterhouseCoopers, 2009, https://www.pwc.com/gx/en/ceo- survey/pdf/pwc_12th_annual_global_ceo_survey_e.pdf, 24.
2. Patrick Lencioni, *The Advantage: Why Organizational Health Trumps Everything Else In Business* (San Francisco: Jossey-Bass, 2012), 94.

3. Marcus Buckingham and Donald O. Clifton, *Now, Discover Your Strengths* (New York: The Free Press, 2001), 8.

4. Jim Collins, *Good to Great: Why Some Companies Make The Leap... And Others Don't* (New York: HarperBusiness, 2001), 41.

5. Heather Boushey and Sarah Jane Glynn, "There Are Significant Costs To Replacing Employees." Center for American Progress, 2012, https://www.americanprogress.org/wp-content/uploads/2012/11/CostofTurnover.pdf.

Chapter 6

1. "Workplace Conflict And How Businesses Can Harness It To Thrive." CPP Inc., 2008, https://www.cpp.com/pdfs/CPP_Global_Human_Capital_Report_Workplace_Conflict.pdf.

Chapter 7

1. Steven Pressfield, *The War of Art: Winning the Inner Creative Battle* (New York: Rugged Land, 2002), 65.

2. Michael Chui et al., "The Social Economy: Unlocking Value and Productivity Through Social Technologies." McKinsey Global Institute, 2012, http://mckinscy.com/industries/high-tech/our-insights/the-social-economy.

3. "Longer Work Days Leave Americans Nodding Off on the Job." National Sleep Foundation, 2008, https://sleepfoundation.org/media-center/press-release/longer-work-days-leave-americans-nodding-the-job.

4. Lymari Morales, "Self-Employed Workers Clock the Most Hours Each Week." Gallup Inc., 2009, http://gallup.com/poll/122510/self-employed-workers-clock-hours-week.aspx.

5. John Pencavel, "The Productivity of Working Hours." Stanford University and Institute for the Study of Labor, 2014, http://ftp.iza.org/dp8129.pdf.

Chapter 10

1. Stephen R. Covey, *The 7 Habits of Highly Effective People* (New York: Simon & Schuster, 1989), 287.

ACKNOWLEDGMENTS

● ● ● ● ● ● ● ● ● ●

I am deeply thankful for the many people who have assisted in bringing this book to completion.

In particular, I want to thank Heidi Grieser, Eric Stutzman, and Wendy Loewen, who read and provided feedback on the manuscript at every step along the way. They are truly contributors to this book; they rewrote sentences, wrote new sentences, and offered general suggestions, most of which I followed.

Thank you to all the staff and trainers at CTRI and ACHIEVE. Without you this book would not exist. Special acknowledgments go to Ana Speranza, who was instrumental in guiding the book through the publishing process, and Reid Hebert, who was ever mindful of the marketing aspects of releasing a book.

I'm grateful for the skill and watchful eyes of my two editors, Ardell Stauffer and Tim Runtz, for my proofreader Joan Padgett, and for the numerous friends who took the time to read through the manuscript and provide feedback. A big thank you to Lisa Friesen. Her creativity resulted in a fabulous book cover and interior design.

To the 10 leaders I interviewed, I am grateful for your insights and the time you gave. Thank you Jeff Schmidt, John Neufeld, Catherine Bargen, Pete Loewen, Carl Heaman-Warne, Shawn McLaren, Joe Grieser, Bob Neufeld, Peter Loewen, and Lynda Monk.

I am very appreciative to the over 1,700 people who participated in the leadership survey referenced throughout the book. Thank you for sharing your insights and opinions.

I am eternally grateful for my parents' support. They have provided me with love and encouragement throughout my life. Finally, my spouse, Heidi, and my children, Ben and Ana – you have put up with my constant thoughts and ponderings about various aspects of this book since the idea emerged. Thank you for your support and patience. I love you.

SPEAKING AND TRAINING

● ● ● ● ● ● ● ● ● ●

Randy Grieser
For your next conference, convention, or leadership retreat, consider having Randy be your speaker. He provides engaging, inspirational, and humorous 30–45 minute keynotes, as well as workshops and retreats.

For more information
www.theordinaryleader.com
info@theordinaryleader.com
877-270-9776

ACHIEVE Centre for Leadership & Workplace Performance
Over 35 workshop topics in the areas of leadership development and workplace performance.

For more information
www.achievecentre.com
info@achievecentre.com
877-270-9776

Crisis & Trauma Resource Institute
Over 40 workshop topics in the areas of counseling, mental health, and violence prevention.

For more information
www.ctrinstitute.com
info@ctrinstitute.com
877-353-3205